The Making of the SCARLET PIMPERNEL

The official companion to the BBC series

GEOFF TIBBALLS
Introduction by Richard E. Grant

BOXTREE

ACKNOWLEDGEMENTS
The author would like to thank the following for their invaluable help in the preparation of this book: Richard E. Grant, Martin Shaw, Elizabeth McGovern, Denise Black, Emilia Fox, Anthony Green, Patrick Lau, Richard Carpenter, Julian Murphy, Tony Virgo, Tim Hutchinson, Howard Burden, Pam Haddock, Terry Walsh, Steve Dent, Wendy Dickinson, Matthew Robinson, Sir Donald Sinden, James Codd at BBC Written Archives and Charlie Carman at Boxtree.

First published 1998 by Boxtree
an imprint of Macmillan Publishers Ltd
25 Eccleston Place · London SW1W 9NF
and Basingstoke

Associated companies throughout the world

ISBN 0 7522 1301 6

A BBC Birmingham/
London Films/A&E Network Production

1 3 5 7 9 8 6 4 2

A CIP catalogue record for this book is available from the British Library

Printed by The Bath Press

Designed by Lovelock & Co.

PICTURE ACKNOWLEDGEMENTS
Whilst every effort has been made to trace copyright holders for photographs featured in this book, we would like to apologise should there have been any errors or omissions. BBC/Sven Arnstein: 4, 26, 50, 57, 59, 63 (bottom), 64, 81, 89, 95, 96, 98, 101, 103, 104, 116, 121 (left), 122; Howard Burden: 78; BBC/Jon Gardey: 2–3, 8, 11, 12–13, 19, 20, 22, 28, 35, 53, 54, 66, 67 (top), 74, 76, 82, 85, 92, 99, 109, 112, 119 (right), 121(right); Tim Hutchinson: 24–5, 70–1, 72, 126–7; BBC/Tony Nutley: 30, 55, 60, 70 (top left), 86, 115, 118; BBC/Zdenek Vavra: 14, 16, 27, 29, 32, 46, 49, 56, 62, 63 (top), 65, 67 (bottom), 68, 69, 70 (top right), 71, 73, 75, 77, 79, 80, 83, 84, 91, 106, 107, 110, 117, 119 (left), 120, 121 (centre), 124, 125; All photographs on the following pages suppled by BFI Stills, Posters and Designs: 36, 38, 39, 40, 41, 42, 43, 44, 45; All photographs on the following pages have been supplied courtesy of Carlton International Media Ltd: 36, 38, 39, 40, 41, 44, 45; All photographs on the following pages have been reproduced courtesy of Warner Bros.:42, 43.

CONTENTS

INTRODUCTION: PIMPERNEL DIARY '98

Richard E. Grant was always the producer's first choice to play the elusive Pimpernel and he joined the team in March 1998. The following extracts were taken from Richard's diaries during filming.

MONDAY 23RD FEBRUARY

Scarlet Pimpernel read-through in the basement of a small West End Hotel. In other words, a 'cannot be avoided' collective panic attack and overheated armpits. Eyeballs swivelling in all directions looking for familiar faces and wondering which will be friends or foe in four months from now? Like the first term at a new school. Followed by a cramped week of costume fittings, horse riding and sword fighting lessons.

SUNDAY 1ST MARCH

Prague – because it looks like eighteenth-century France (and it's much cheaper than shooting in England). Sunday night. Forum Hotel: cocooned on the 22nd floor. Or wind tornado epicentral, feeling isolated and sorry for myself. Channel surf through East European soap operas and discussions – everyone looks like they're fresh from 1972. A BBC assistant rings – 'Is everything alright?' I dare not tell her.

MONDAY 2ND MARCH

6.00 a.m. alarm call due. For 6.50 pick up. Only there isn't one. Wake at 6.45 and move from horizontal to perpendicular in seconds. Shave, shower and steam into the foyer in four and half minutes flat. Into the car and stretch my three Czech words into a half-hour conversation with the smiling driver whom I suspect hasn't a clue what I'm talking about. Into make-up and breeches and enough buttons to service a panto.

Down into an eighteenth-century torture chamber: smoke, chains, fake blood and non-English speaking jailers. Terry Walsh, the calm, patient, fight and stunt arranger, has the task of making me look like I could kill someone. Curiously, nobody laughs. Our director, Patrick Lau, is all encouraging.

James Bond 'Q' activities: a lock-pick is hidden in my eyeglass to escape my cell, a sword in a secret boot compartment. Handle hidden in false heel. *Boys' Own* stuff. Learn to swear proficiently in Czech.

I am required to come hurtling around a corner, bound up the stairs and dispose of a horde of revolutionaries. My stunt double, George, skinnier than me, doesn't seem at all fazed and eins, zwei, drei, and he cuts, thrusts and swathes his way through them all. Then it's my turn to step in for some close-up *coup-de-grace* sword work. Do the first slice and feel like a perfumed ponce. Then watch the playback monitor and lo and withhold my breath, but it does look as if I have actually done the dirty deed.

SATURDAY 7TH MARCH

Stunt double exploded through a window for me, then I

took over and ran up a cobbled street. All day.

Saturday night at the end of the first week and we are on schedule, thanks to Patrick Lau's precise and well-prepared directions. No messing about.

TUESDAY 10TH MARCH

Dinner with Emilia Fox, Jamie Bamber and Pascale Langdale swapping stories of casting humiliations. The menu offers up 'Old Deer'. Of which there are a couple at an adjacent table.

WEDNESDAY 11TH MARCH

SNOGGING AND SNOW

Prague looks like its own daguerreotype advert.

First day with Elizabeth McGovern. My 'wife'. Our characters meet in frosty mode then melt into a passionate snog. Breath alert: floss, scrub, swarfega, buff, check, double-check, saliva sample for stray pongs, before tongues away. Surrounded by forty technicians cramped in a cell. Mmmmmmmm!

SATURDAY 14TH MARCH

Spent the afternoon in bed with Elizabeth. Aboard ship. Sir Percy and his wife in intimate mode.

Vashek, my driver is a committed Boney M fan and I have been subjected to daily doses of 'RA RA RASPUTIN', and am thinking of persuading him that his Celine Dion CD might be the lesser of these two aural evils.

MONDAY 30TH MARCH

Scene features dancers doing a routine where they wobble their heads about as though about to lose them to the guillotine. The Italian choreographer is a cousin of Fronck, the wedding co-ordinator in *Father of the Bride*.

WEDNESDAY 1ST APRIL

Back to Prague. Aaah the perfume of pollution, traffic congestion and city life. Three days of the Czech countryside are a lifetime's worth.

'SUITS YOU, SIR!' from *The Fast Show* has become word game play with the English crew, transforming any and every conversation or banal aside into a sexually loaded double entendre, 'radiant, moist, tight, fitted, gusseted and gagging', get us through the long days.

MONDAY 6TH APRIL – EPISODE TWO

The reality of only having eleven working days in England, in a four-month schedule based in the Czech republic, is taking its toll on the general sanity levels. Lopsiding proceedings.

WEDNESDAY 22ND APRIL

Night shoot it is. Sleep through the morning and go to work at 3.30 p.m. Krivoklat Castle. An hour's drive out of Prague.

Pam Haddock, make-up chief is in a state – having had someone enter her locked bedroom in the Forum Hotel in the middle of the night. She screamed. He sauntered out in his cashmere coat. Leaving her boots outside the door. She is terrified. Hotel security didn't call the police, but instead offered up a picture of someone asking, 'Is this the man?' Pam is moved to another room and we are all committed to bolting the doors and barricading them with chairs just for safety.

FRIDAY 24TH APRIL

Radost nightclub with cast and make-up crew. Evening enlivened by a pipe-cleaner-skinny Belgian clubber who intro'd himself, topless, pierced and welded into second-skin shiny PVC trousers. This nocturnal venturer is a military airline mechanic, speaks four languages, had dropped two Es and was very chatty. He explained that the four different-sized metal rings chained to his pocket were for encircling his genitalia 'for presentation purposes'.

SATURDAY 25TH APRIL

Home for a getaway break. Airport procedures at Prague require much looking and snorting at passport details, extensive metal-detector body searching and the unmistakeable impression that the officials hanker for a touch of the old KGBs. Took my levitating nine-year-old daughter to the Spice Girls concert – two and a half hours of smoke, song, dance, scream, space effects, video, singalong, audience participation and 20,000 pre-teens going AWOL. Remembered that I got *The Sound of Music* soundtrack at the same age.

TUESDAY 28TH APRIL

Zatec. Location an hour's drive out of Prague and huge crowds of extras, smoke, fire, horses, guillotine and mayhem, sword fighting and stunts – oh, and a couple of journalists requiring some hubbly-bubbly talk.

It's an odd dilemma to be explaining yourself in the midst of doing the role and I hear the following words assembling themselves: 'Well, Sir Percy is in the tradition of all double-life heroes. A kind of eighteenth-century Bruce Wayne/Batman, Clark Kent/Superman, with a perfumed ponce persona that hides an heroic clandestine life. A man living by his wits, an adrenaline 'junkie', with a Beau Brummel predilection for a chi-chi wardrobe'.

The producers and director took the decision not to attempt elaborate prosthetic disguises and to rely on Percy's wit, speed and guile to get him in and out of scrapes.

MONDAY 4TH MAY

Barrendov Studios. Loss of confidence as to how to go for the fop. Takes a while and went home feeling tail between legs, but knowing that this has to be embraced full pelt if it is to work.

SUNDAY 10TH MAY

Two weeks of sanity in England. I felt like a returning Pope ready to kiss some tarmac. Everything looked and smelt and felt all things bright and beautiful. Nothing to translate. Choice. Choice beyond description. The sheer relief to be on home turf and real life.

TUESDAY 26TH MAY

THE RETURN. THE FINAL HAUL. New director – Ed Bennett. The ep. reads fast and clear.

Elizabeth poses the question that cannot be asked – 'Why don't Chauvelin and Robespierre just arrest or execute Percy?'

Suzanne Bertish, playing the transvestite villain, was to be heard bellowing at 4 a.m. – 'Does *anyone* speak English here?' (The hotel in the middle of nowhere was 'undergoing completion'.) 'HOT WATER?!' The blank incomprehension of the night staff was more than matched by her increasing rage.

TUESDAY 23RD JUNE

'Please release me, let me go' has become our anthem, prompted by the fact that it has been at number one in the Prague pop chart for two months, sung by one Lucie Bila. Her rendition replete with Baroque orgasmic shrieks and swoops which match the mounting hysteria and mood swings of the English crew.

Things got truly surreal post a dice-playing scene. A large group of adults stood around a card table, watching and endlessly filming my hand in close-up, rolling dice in an attempt to get the scripted numbers to come up. Someone pointed out that we had as much chance of winning the lottery. However, after forty minutes or so, the right combinations had asserted themselves and with it the very real prospect of going home. What began in thermals and coats midwinter was coming to a conclusion in T-shirts in midsummer. How would we get through our futures without hearing these familiar words – 'skoshka' (rehearsal) and 'more smoke please' (so beloved of lighting cameramen)? Possibly in one of the fleet of Skodas put-putting across the countryside...

Percy was here

CHAPTER ONE

VIVE LA REVOLUTION

The French Revolution of 1789 was gunpowder. When it was lit, the blast rocked Europe. It was a time of courage and cruelty, of heroes and villains, and one which Baroness Emmuska Orczy saw as the perfect setting for the daring exploits of her fictional knight in shining armour, the Scarlet Pimpernel.

The seeds of discontent which led to the French Revolution had been sown centuries before with a social system which not only made the nobility a privileged class, but largely exempted it from taxation. In common with most of Europe, the ordinary people remained oppressed by feudal burdens which had been in existence since the Middle Ages. They were little more than serfs, subject to harsh punishments if they ever stepped out of line. Such a set-up suited the nobles and also the Church which taught that man, through Adam's sin, was naturally evil and utterly incapable of devising a better social system. At the start of the eighteenth century, these conditions prevailed in France because nobody had the courage to challenge them, but gradually radical philosophers emerged who were not afraid to air their views. The Church, the monarchy and the nobles were alarmed that their absolute power might be threatened by these new ideas. A little learning might prove a dangerous thing.

In 1726 the French writer François Voltaire visited England and was struck by how things differed from his homeland. Under the Hanoverian kings, royal power was curbed by an elected parliament and there was no arbitrary taxation: nobles and clerics alike were obliged to pay. Furthermore, whereas in France free speech was banned, the English people were allowed a degree of liberty to speak, write and worship as they wished. To Voltaire's observant mind, the English seemed a much happier race than their French counterparts. On his return to France, Voltaire voiced his ideas for reform, being particularly critical of the higher clergy whom he scathingly denounced as intolerant enemies of progress. In his *Lettres philosophiques*, Voltaire spread the word of scientist Isaac Newton and of John Locke, the English philosopher who, among

The towering guillotine – the most feared sight in Revolutionary France.

other things, advocated the overthrow of a government if it infringed such fundamental rights as religious freedom. Although Voltaire's works were banned and publicly burnt by the French authorities, they still sold remarkably well and, as his teachings spread, they were taken up by new writers, most notably Jean-Jacques Rousseau who, in 1762, published his *Du contrat social.* Rousseau's social contract proclaimed that the principle of good government was based on the will of the people, with every citizen sacrificing his personal interests in favour of the welfare of the community.

The War of the Austrian Succession (1740–48) and the Seven Years War (1756–63) had drained France economically and by the time Louis XVI ascended the throne in 1774, the country was in a bad way. The situation was not helped by the king's frivolous wife, Marie Antoinette, whose arrogance and love of the good life led to her being resented at court and hated by the people. In 1778, France, keen to compensate for her territorial losses to Britain as a result of the Seven Years War, sided with the American colonies in the War of Independence. The revenge gained at Britain's expense was sweet but it also cost France a lot of money. Additionally, the colonists' triumph served to fuel the fires of liberty which were burning among the French people.

The freedom movement gained momentum almost on a daily basis. While the autocratic Louis could tax, imprison or silence his subjects at will and the favoured nobles idled their time away at Versailles, the hard-working middle classes and the humble peasants bridled at the system of privilege and the unfair burden of taxation which was imposed upon them. Many peasants had to surrender three-quarters of their earnings to the State and their local lords. The gulf between the upper and lower echelons of French society had never been wider. The monarchy, nobility and senior clergy had forfeited all respect and, unlike in England, there was no national parliament to air the country's grievances. The nearest equivalent, the Estates-General – an assembly of clergy, nobles and bourgeoisie – had not been summoned since 1614.

With the nation in such a perilous state financially, one thing that was needed above all else was a bumper harvest. So the freak storm which swept across northern France on 13 July 1788, carrying hailstones so big that they killed men and livestock and devastated hundreds of square miles of crops just as harvest was approaching, came as a wound to the heart of the economy. Even in regions unaffected by the storm, the yield was poor, as a result of the long spring drought which had failed to swell the grain. These summer disasters were followed by the coldest winter within living memory. Northern France was in the grip of arctic weather from December to April, while in Provence and Languedoc thousands of tender vines and olive trees were destroyed by the severe frosts. The dismal harvest saw bread prices rocket – a crippling blow to the average French family. With the government bankrupt and the nobles and clergy firmly resisting any plans to tax them, Louis decided to convene the old Estates-General for 5 May 1789. Two weeks before the assembly met, rioters took to the streets of Paris to

storm the house of wallpaper manufacturer Reveillon, whose remark that the price of bread should be lowered to levels affordable for the lower classes was misinterpreted as a call for wage reductions. A detachment of the French Guards was brought in to quell the riot, leaving twenty-five dead. Rumours put the number considerably higher.

The Revolution was partly sparked by the insensitivity of Marie Antoinette. When told that the people were short of bread, she famously replied: 'Let them eat cake.'

The meeting of the Estates-General was a tension-packed affair with deadlock between the Church, the nobility and the 'third estate' which comprised the rest of the nation but chiefly represented the bourgeoisie. The privileged orders refused to co-operate with the commoners, whereupon the latter broke away and formed a National Assembly, vowing that they would never separate until they had given France a new constitution. The lesser nobility and the rural clergy supported them, and soon the king, yielding to the swell of public opinion, ordered the other groups to join the Assembly.

Meanwhile the atmosphere in Paris was electric. Fearful for her own safety, Marie Antoinette persuaded Louis to place a body of troops on stand-by. Immediately the cry went up that the Assembly was in peril and the people took up arms. On 14 July a lawless mob, armed with pike and cannon, stormed the Bastille, the grim state prison which they saw as a symbol of royal tyranny. Over a hundred people perished but the Bastille surrendered. For the mob, it was a famous victory.

Overleaf: Angry, hungry mobs storm Paris in search of royalist sympathisers.

The triumphant citizens set up a municipal government and recruited a National Guard. The humiliated Louis was forced to sanction these measures and to wear in his

A revolutionary tribunal sits in judgement, under the leadership of the sinister Fumier (right, played by Chris Fairbank).

royal hat the revolutionary tricolour cockade of red, white and blue. Bread riots spread throughout France and, as their castles were razed to the ground, many nobles fled abroad in search of foreign assistance to help quash the rebellions. By October, the mistrust of the monarchy resurfaced in a fresh outbreak of violence. A hungry mob, some 7,000 strong, invaded the Palace of Versailles, forcing the king and queen to move to the Tuileries palace in the capital. The National Assembly resumed its sittings nearby and continued its task of thrashing out France's new constitution. One of its first acts was the Declaration of the Rights of Man, which asserted the claim of all citizens to liberty, equality, justice and a voice in legislation and taxation. 'Liberty, Equality, Fraternity' became the rallying call of the Revolution.

Two years later, the measures were completed. A limited monarchy was created, along with a Legislative Assembly to be elected by all except the poorer classes. The privileges of the nobility were abolished and the vast estates of the Church were confiscated; bishops and parish priests became salaried civil servants, elected by the people without consulting the Pope.

The new constitution may have swept away centuries of social abuse but it also created fresh divisions. The civil appointment of the clergy stunned devout Catholics. The majority of the bishops and half of the parish priests resigned in protest and declared the Revolution to be an enemy of religion. And the poorer commoners, who already suspected that the bourgeoisie were using the Assembly to further their own ends, were angry at being excluded from parliamentary elections and at the apparent neglect of their economic problems.

Meanwhile Louis and his queen were up to no good. As an army of emigrant French nobles formed across the Rhine in Prussia, Louis began secret negotiations with that country and with the Austrian emperor, Marie Antoinette's brother. In June 1791, the double-dealing Louis, heavily disguised, made a dash for the border, with the apparent intention of returning to Paris at the head of an Austrian army. But his carriage was stopped at Varennes and Louis and Marie Antoinette were swiftly taken back to the Tuileries, where the populace could keep an eye on them. The abortive flight hardened feelings against the king, who was denounced as a traitor. At the same time, the inflamed masses were clamouring for still more radical measures, in opposition to the moderate bourgeoisie who were content with the reforms already achieved.

In October 1791, when the new Legislative Assembly (successor to the National Assembly) met for the first time, a division grew between moderate Girondists and radical Jacobins. The Girondists (so named because a number of their leaders came from the Gironde region) formed a government but almost immediately faced threats from within (the Jacobins) and without (Austria and Prussia). These two countries announced their intention to restore Louis's authority whereupon, in April 1792, France declared war.

By August the treacherous Louis had shown that his sympathies lay with the enemy rather than his own country. The charismatic orator and Jacobin leader Georges Danton whipped the populace into a frenzy and organised an uprising which ended with the Tuileries palace being stormed and the king taken prisoner. As news arrived that Prussian troops were on French soil, the paranoia in Paris reached fever pitch. Danton saw traitors everywhere and demanded a sweeping search of all homes in the capital for possible suspects. As a result, some 3,000 people were thrown into the prisons of Paris, unsure of their fate.

The overthrow of the monarchy brought the more extreme Jacobins to the fore, notably the lawyer Maximilien François Marie Isidore de Robespierre and journalist Jean Paul Marat, the self-styled friend of the people but a man who had previously been considered too bloodthirsty to command popular support. Now Marat came into his own. His solution to the growing crisis was to suggest the massacre both of the suspects in the prisons and of selected ministers and deputies. On 2 September, the Prussians took Verdun, the final fortress on the road to Paris. In another rousing speech, Danton urged his compatriots: 'If we are bold, bolder still, and forever bold, then France is saved!' But the mood in Paris was one of panic. That afternoon, a convoy of prisoners was stopped and attacked by sansculottes, as the revolutionaries were known because they preferred to wear trousers rather than the aristocracy's breeches. Seventeen prisoners were hacked to death but this was only the start of the butchery. Between 2 and 7 September over 1,000 royalists and alleged traitors were executed in the September Massacres. Few of the victims were politically dangerous but the killings satisfied the blood-lust of Marat and his followers – at least for the time being.

On 22 September, a Jacobin-dominated National Convention formally abolished the monarchy and proclaimed France a republic. While the raw French soldiers, singing their new war song 'La Marseillaise', were forcing the Prussian armies back, the king was tried for treason and condemned to death. The initial proposal for a device 'to make heads fly off in the twinkling of an eye' had been greeted with ridicule by the Assembly back in 1789, but the campaign by Dr Joseph Ignace Guillotin in support of the machine developed by his friend, Antoine Louis, eventually proved successful. The device was given the good doctor's name in 1792 and, on 25 April that year, it claimed its first victim – a highwayman. Now it was to claim its most famous victim -- the deposed King of France.

The trial of Louis XVI before the National Convention in December was little more than a formality. Robespierre firmly opposed the idea of giving the king a fair hearing, declaring that he had already been tried and found guilty by the people: 'Louis cannot be judged, he has already been judged. He has been condemned, or else the Republic is not blameless. To suggest putting Louis XVI on trial, in whatever way, is a step backwards towards royal and constitutional despotism; it is a counter-revolutionary idea; because it puts the Revolution itself in the dock. After all, if Louis can still be put on trial, Louis can be acquitted; he might be innocent. Or rather, he is presumed to be until he is found guilty. But if Louis is acquitted, if Louis can be presumed innocent, what becomes of the Revolution?'

As the fighting grew ever more fierce, 1,000 royalists and suspected traitors were executed in the notorious September Massacres.

Nevertheless, the decision to execute the king was not taken lightly. At his brief trial Louis was allowed – albeit reluctantly – a defending counsel who portrayed his client more as a victim of circumstance than a scheming tyrant, someone who had acceded to the wishes of the people by granting them liberty. And whilst it was inevitable that he would be found guilty, the debate over whether to execute or reprieve him raged from the moment the king was escorted from the chamber. The Girondins favoured clemency while the hard-liners saw death as the only sentence. Ultimately, it was the dread of reprisals that probably sealed Louis's fate, for there were widespread fears that if the king was spared, the sansculottes would take to the streets and massacre those responsible for his reprieve. The final Convention vote in January was certainly close: 361 for immediate execution; 72 for the death penalty, but only after a suitable delay; and 288 for imprisonment. On the following day, 18 January 1793, after the decision had been relayed to the king, a reprieve was proposed and another vote was taken. This time 310 opposed execution, but 380 were still in favour of carrying out the sentence. There were to be no further delays and, on Monday 21 January, Louis went to the guillotine, his final protestations of innocence drowned out by rolling drums.

The death of Louis XVI sent shock waves through the rest of Europe. Whereas many prominent Englishmen had welcomed the fall of the Bastille – politician Charles James Fox had hailed it as 'the greatest and best event in history' and even the poet William Wordsworth had temporarily forsaken thoughts of golden daffodils to sing its praises – Britain was now alarmed at the act of regicide and at the French occupation of Belgium. A coalition comprising Britain, Holland, Austria, Prussia, Spain and Sardinia was formed against France and, in March, the French were driven out of Belgium. The French General Charles Dumouriez deserted to the enemy. The road to Paris lay open.

The following month, the National Convention delegated power to a Committee of Public Safety, led by the incorruptible Robespierre, a man said to have once declined an appointment as a judge because he could not face the idea of passing the death sentence. Events would soon show that he had overcome his scruples. The moderate Girondins were overthrown as the Jacobins seized power, supported by the Paris mob. In July, the Girondins gained some revenge when their most ferocious adversary, Marat, was stabbed to death in his bath by Charlotte Corday. She was duly guillotined four days later.

Under siege from all sides, France rallied once more and forced the foreign invaders to retreat. By 1794, the Austrians had been driven from Belgium and the French had occupied Holland.

While the French army was routing its foes, the government carried out a mass purge of those considered to be traitors to the cause. Inspired by the teachings of Rousseau, the self-righteous Robespierre visualised a 'Republic of Virtue' governed by the concepts of humanitarianism, social idealism and patriotism. He pursued this goal with merciless, unwavering zeal, denouncing all opponents as traitors. For ten months from 5 September 1793 until 27 July 1794, Robespierre's Reign of Terror rooted out all enemies, real or imaginary. One of its first pieces of legislation was the Law of Suspects which empowered watch committees set up the previous March to arrest anyone who 'either by their conduct, their words or their writings, showed themselves to be supporters of tyranny, of federalism, or to be enemies of liberty'. It also allowed for the arrest of various other categories, such as former nobles 'who have not constantly manifested their attachment to the Revolution'. This gave Robespierre and his red-capped henchmen plenty of scope. Even those who addressed each other as 'Monsieur' instead of the sansculotte 'citizen' fell under automatic suspicion.

The Reign of Terror's most famous victim was Marie Antoinette, who had been kept in solitary confinement following the execution of her husband. When news broke of a plot to free her, she was hastily tried for treason and, in the wake of the inevitable guilty verdict, she was led defiantly to the guillotine on 17 October. Two weeks later, twenty-one Girondins met a similar fate and the most familiar sight in the streets of Paris and other French towns became that of the tumbril, the two-wheeled cart taking hordes of prisoners destined, in the words of Baroness Orczy, 'for the fond embrace of Madame la Guillotine'. So brisk was the trade in Paris that the guillotine acquired a permanent site, close to where Louis XVI's head had fallen in La Place de la Révolution (now La Place de la Concorde).

Yet although Paris boasted the most celebrated victims of the guillotine, it could not claim the most ruthless revolutionary tribunal. That dubious distinction went to Nantes, where supporters of a Catholic and royalist rebellion in the Vendée were dealt with. Having failed to capture Nantes itself, the rebels retreated into the Vendéan heartland, pursued by Republican armies. The rebels tried to link up with the British at Granville, on the Cotentin peninsula opposite Jersey, but the British warships failed to arrive in time. Forced to flee south, the rebels were confronted at Le Mans. The Republican commander offered no mercy. 'The road to Laval is strewn with corpses,' reported one of his men. 'Women, priests, monks, children, all have been put to death. I have spared nobody.' Estimates put the death toll at 10,000. On 23 December, the final remnants of the rebel army turned to face its pursuers at Savenay. No more than 5,000 were in a fit state to fight although twice that number crammed into the little town. Two-thirds of them were killed in the battle and the mass shootings which followed. The Great War of the Vendée was over.

In the space of just three months, the Nantes tribunal sent over 8,000 people to the guillotine, yet still the prisons were overflowing and ravaged by disease. There was insufficient food to cater for innocent citizens, let alone condemned traitors and rebels, and so the republicans devised a new method of disposal. On 19 November, some 90

priests were executed by sinking them, tied together, in a holed barge in the Loire. In the ensuing six weeks, a further six batches of victims (many of them priests suspected of encouraging the rebels) were dispatched in the same way. The bodies were washed up on the tidal banks of the Loire for weeks afterwards.

In just three months in 1793, the Nantes revolutionary tribunal sent over 8,000 people to the guillotine.

In the meantime, France was distancing itself yet further from the established Church. In October 1793, a new republican calendar was introduced under which years would no longer be numbered from the birth of Christ, but from the inauguration of the French Republic on 22 September 1792. There would be twelve thirty-day months given appropriate seasonal names, such as *Pluviôse* (rain) for January–February and *Thermidor* (heat) for July–August. Each month would have three ten-day weeks ending in a rest day or *décadi*. Therefore Sundays disappeared and could only be observed if they coincided with the rest days. In November 1793, all churches in Paris were closed, soon followed by the rest of France. The divorce from the Church was all but complete.

Although there was a temporary fall in the number of executions, the Reign of Terror continued to claim illustrious casualties. Danton fell foul of the fanatical Robespierre for suggesting an end to the executions and, on 5 April 1794, went to the guillotine himself. His death marked the beginning of a new phase in the Terror, when

The tricolour cockade of red, white and blue became a symbol of the French Revolution.

people would die for crimes they might commit as much as for those they had committed, and sometimes simply because they failed to match Robespierre's high moral standards. Robespierre noted solemnly: 'The word virtue made Danton laugh. How could a man, to whom all idea of morality was foreign, be the defender of liberty?'

The Terror had a sting in its tail, especially in Paris. The purpose of the tribunal was redefined as the punishment of enemies of the people, and the only penalty it was allowed to impose was death. As a result, the carnage increased dramatically. In June and July, 1,515 people were guillotined in Paris, many of them nobles, clerics and the richer bourgeoisie. Indeed 38 per cent of Paris's noble victims, 26 per cent of its clerical and almost half of the wealthier middle-class ones were executed during this short but bloody period.

But the tide was beginning to turn against Robespierre. There were dark mutterings that he was becoming a dictator and when he appeared at the head of a religious procession, the Festival of the Supreme Being, as part of the new policy to reverse the dechristianisation of France, one of Danton's former associates remarked icily: 'It's not enough for him to be master, he has to be God.' Robespierre, whose warped sense of humour extended to having guillotine designs on his buttons, had already survived one assassination attempt but the forces against him were gathering. As his determination to purge spread even to the Committee of Public Safety itself, many of his former allies feared that they would be next for the chop. It seemed that nobody was safe from Robespierre's paranoia. On 27 July, when he rose to speak at the National Convention the day after delivering a long speech in which he appeared to threaten just about everybody, he was drowned out by cries of 'Down with the tyrant!' He was repeatedly refused the floor while a series of attacks was launched on his behaviour. Finally he was arrested, along with his brother Augustin and a few of his closest associates, including Louis de Saint-Just.

Although Robespierre had fatally overestimated his support among the deputies, the influential Paris commune stood by him and ordered all jailers in the capital to refuse to accept the prisoners. One, François Hanriot, commander of the Paris National Guard, was allowed to escape in order to muster support while Robespierre and the others were given sanctuary by the commune at the Hôtel de Ville. But the National Guard did not respond to Hanriot's call and when the Convention ruled that the prisoners, presumed to have escaped, were outlawed, the outlook for Robespierre and his followers was bleak. For, under a law first proposed, ironically, by Saint-Just, this meant that they could be executed without trial. Under the leadership of Paul, Viscount de Barras, troops arrived at the Hôtel de Ville at two o'clock on the morning of 29 July. The hotel was undefended. Sensing the inevitable, Robespierre had tried to shoot himself but had merely succeeded in breaking his jaw. It was heavily bandaged to stop it hanging off when he was led to the guillotine the following afternoon. He was just thirty-three years old. His brother, Saint-Just and eighty of Robespierre's closest disciples followed him to the scaffold over the next twenty-four hours. The grisly spectacle was witnessed by Irish political exile Hamilton Rowan, who wrote: 'About sixty persons were guillotined in less than one hour and a half, in the Place de la Révolution; and though I was standing above a hundred paces from the place of execution, the blood of the victims streamed beneath my feet. What surprised me was, as each head fell into the basket, the cry of the people was no other than a repetition of "*A bas le Maximum*!"'

The overthrow of Robespierre brought an end to the Reign of Terror. The guillotine alone had claimed 17,000 victims throughout France but, coupled with those who died in prison or on the field of conflict, the death toll of the Terror reached around 40,000. Of those condemned by the revolutionary tribunals, only 8 per cent were nobles, 6 per cent were clergy, 14 per cent were middle class and a staggering 70 per cent were workers or peasants, charged with such crimes as draft dodging, desertion, hoarding and rebellion. So the commonly held belief that the principal victims of the Revolution were the aristocracy is not strictly true. The poor commoners, supposedly the instigators of the uprising, suffered infinitely greater losses.

As the country sickened of the red tyranny, the Paris commune was abolished and the Jacobin Club closed. In 1795, moderate Thermidoreans took control of the National Convention and created a new executive Directory of five members. Established to hold a middle course between royalism and Jacobinism, the Directory ruled France for four years but proved hopelessly corrupt and inefficient. Moreover, the aggressive wars in which it engaged led to the formation of another coalition of European powers. The one person to emerge from these campaigns covered in glory was a young general by the name of Napoleon Bonaparte and when a coup d'état overthrew the Directory in 1799, Napoleon was made Chief Consul with practically supreme power. Thus the Revolution acquired a new dictator.

Despite its barbaric nature, the French Revolution achieved worthy goals. The unfair and outdated privileges of the nobility and the clergy were buried too deeply ever to be resurrected, while the spirit of individual freedom, political liberty and equal justice lived on and soon spread to neighbouring countries. France had set a standard which the rest of Europe would follow.

CHAPTER TWO

THE LIFE AND TIMES OF BARONESS ORCZY

Emma Magdalena Rosalia Maria Josefa Barbara Orczy was born on 22 September 1865 at Tarna-Eörs in Hungary, the only child of Baron Felix Orczy, the noted composer and conductor, and Emma Orczy, née Comtesse Wass. Her upbringing revolved around music and, through her father, she knew such celebrated composers as Richard Wagner, Franz Liszt, Charles François Gounod and Jules Massenet. The Baron was something of an innovator, often ahead of his time, and when he attempted to introduce modern farming methods to his little corner of Hungary, the suspicious local peasants reacted by setting his crops and buildings on fire. This unrest forced him to surrender his holding and, with his daughter still a little girl, the family felt obliged to flee the country.

It was naturally assumed – and hoped – that Emma (or Emmuska as she came to be known) would follow in her father's footsteps, and her family's wealth enabled her to study music in Brussels and Paris. 'Before I reached my teens, I could already jabber in three languages without a trace of a foreign accent,' she remarked. At the age of fifteen she moved to London with her family. Remarkably for someone who went on to write solely in English, she didn't even speak the language until then.

In London, her interest in a career in music steadily waned and instead she turned her thoughts to art, choosing to study at the West London School of Art. She then enrolled at the Heatherley School of Art where she met a fellow student, Montagu Barstow, the son of a Yorkshire clergyman. He swept her off her feet and they married in 1894, the start of a long and happy union. In her 1947 autobiography, *Links in the Chain of Life*, she wrote: 'My marriage was for close on half a century one of perfect happiness and understanding, of perfect friendship and communion of thought. The

The quills with which the Pimpernel wrote the notes that spread fear into the hearts of his republican adversaries.

great link in my chain of life which brought me everything that makes life worth the living.'

Soon after the wedding, the happy couple went to live in Paris before travelling extensively around Europe. He became an established artist while she too enjoyed modest success as an illustrator and they began to work together on book and magazine illustrations. She also had three paintings hung in London's Royal Academy.

In 1899 their only son, John Montagu Orczy Barstow, was born. He went on to become professor of English at Lausanne and to write under the name of 'John Blakeney', a derivation all too obvious to devotees of *The Scarlet Pimpernel.*

By then, she had become convinced that she wasn't destined to be a painter after all, and decided instead to take up writing while staying in London as the paying guest of a family whose two daughters penned stories for magazines. She thought these young girls knew nothing of the world whereas she, with her knowledge broadened by travel, was sure she could improve on their efforts. She began writing in the late 1890s, composing short stories for the popular magazines of the day.

She met with immediate success and, in 1899, sold 'Juliette' to the *Royal Magazine.* Her early efforts were moderately popular but not enough to make her a fortune. Indeed writing proved to be more difficult than she had thought and she struggled to find a market until the editor of the Pearson magazines suggested that she might profit from the success of Sir Arthur Conan Doyle's recently published Sherlock Holmes adventures by writing a series of detective stories.

The result was 'The Old Man in the Corner', which introduced one of the first armchair detectives. The premise is that the Old Man whiles away his time sitting in a cheap restaurant frequented by journalists. He starts talking to Polly Burton, a young newspaperwoman with whom he has struck up a casual acquaintance, and, by focusing on the crime reports in the papers, somehow manages to come up with a solution which has hitherto eluded the police. The emphasis is very much on the denouement rather than the crime itself or the subsequent police investigation. And all the time he is showing the police the error of their ways, the Old Man plays with a bit of string which he ties into elaborate knots. One critic described the Old Man as 'the nameless logician who sits, shabby and indifferent, at his café table and holds penetrating post-mortems on the crimes of the day'. Another, looking back on the history of detective

Production designer Tim Hutchinson's drawing of the set for Minette's bedroom which features in episode one.

fiction, found him to be 'an early example of the intuitive school of detectives which has become better known in G.K. Chesterton's *Father Brown*'.

Baroness Orczy wrote a total of thirty-eight stories about the Old Man and Polly, the first appearing in the *Royal Magazine* between 1901 and 1904. The first two series of stories were combined and published in book form as *The Old Man in the Corner* in 1909. The third series appeared in book form as *The Case of Miss Elliott* and the fourth series as *Unravelled Knots* in 1926. This last collection proved less successful than its predecessors but to this day the Old Man's tales are of considerable historical interest.

Meanwhile the Baroness had experienced a vision. It was a vision of a character which was to dominate her life and spread her fame throughout the literary world. It was a vision of Sir Percy Blakeney, alias the Scarlet Pimpernel. Creative people can have visions in the most unlikely places but even the Baroness conceded that the west-bound platform of London Underground's Temple station was highly improbable.

'Of all the dull, prosy, uninspiring places in the world,' she asked, 'can you beat a London Underground Station on a dreary, foggy November afternoon? I had gone to meet the editor of the *Daily Express* who, knowing of my work for romantic magazines, suggested I write a story which could run as a serial in his paper. I was immensely flattered by the suggestion but I had practically no experience in the writing of a novel, let alone a romantic one. Somewhat despondently, I made my way back towards home which was in Kensington.

'While waiting for my Inner Circle train, I saw Sir Percy Blakeney just as you know him now. I saw him in his exquisite clothes, his slender hands holding up his spy-glass: I heard his lazy drawling speech, his quaint laugh.' It was a purely mental vision and lasted only a few seconds but 'it was the whole life story of the Scarlet Pimpernel that was there and then revealed to me'.

Opposite: Heavily disguised but led by Sir Percy, the League of the Pimpernel perform another daring rescue.

Arriving home, she could hardly wait to tell her husband. She was so overwhelmed and excited by her new idea that she later recalled not being able to remember anything else that had happened that day. The thing which particularly appealed to her was the opportunity to lift the public from what she perceived as the drabness of their everyday existence. In her memoirs she wrote, 'Rich or poor, life was all the same: so often drab and monotonous and I had thought I would give them romance, stories of the past that would bring back to their minds happy days of youth and carefree adolescence, love, laughter, adventure, gaiety.'

Below: Baroness Orczy described Marguerite (played by Elizabeth McGovern) as one of the most beautiful and intelligent women in Europe.

The Baroness's story first appeared in 1900 entitled 'The Red Carnation'. It was set in contemporary Russia and, three years later, was serialised in the *Daily Express* under the heading 'The Sign of the Shamrock'.

Before it appeared in serial form, she decided while staying in Paris, a city she knew so well, to make drastic alterations for a novel version of the story. The most obvious was to switch the setting from modern Russia to eighteenth-century France, at the time of the Revolution. She also swapped flowers, the red carnation becoming the more romantic-sounding scarlet pimpernel. And it was with this little red star-shaped flower that her dashing English hero would sign his provocative notes to the French Public Prosecutor...every time a royalist escaped to England from the jaws of the guillotine.

Baroness Orczy knew that the success of the book would depend on her central character. 'I remember Arnold Bennett saying once to me: "A book will live by the characters that

people its story, characters that make the story real; it will never live by the story alone, however well constructed or interesting it may be."' So she concentrated on creating a strong 'live outstanding personality' and, to this end, invested him with a double life as Sir Percy and the Scarlet Pimpernel.

'In the same way as I originally saw my Sir Percy Blakeney on the platform of a railway station, so did I see the seething mobs in the Paris of the Revolution, the tumbrils, the guillotine, the prisoners in the Conciergerie, the Scarlet Pimpernel plotting and planning for their release; I saw him in his various disguises, I saw him feigning sleep at midnight at Lord Grenville's ball with Chauvelin vaguely puzzled at first, then with the dawn of comprehension lighting up his thin sallow face.' She found that to transcribe these pictures with her pen was 'a comparatively simple matter' and wrote all thirty-one chapters of *The Scarlet Pimpernel* in just five weeks in 1902.

The action in Baroness Orczy's novel begins in September 1792 with the description of 'a surging, seething, murmuring crowd of beings that are human only in name, for to the eye and ear they seem naught but savage creatures, animated by vile passions and by the lust of vengeance and of hate'. As she goes on to describe the guillotine as a 'hideous instrument of torture' which 'would finally demand the head of a King and of a beautiful young Queen', it quickly becomes apparent where the author's sympathies lie. To her, Marie Antoinette is an innocent victim of the mob rather than a vain wastrel whose arrogance and insensitivity did much to spark the Revolution in the first place.

The Pimpernel taunted his enemies with notes, all signed with the distinctive flower.

The story is set in France and England, in locations such as Paris, Dover, Richmond and Calais, and centres on a mysterious Englishman known as the Scarlet Pimpernel who, together with his small band of dedicated followers (the League of the Scarlet Pimpernel), has devoted his energies and risked his neck to spring innocent French aristocrats from the horror of the guillotine by means of a succession of daring plots and disguises. The notes signed with the scarlet pimpernel flower are said to be the only things that frighten the ruthless Citoyen Foucquier-Tinville who presides over the notorious Committee of Public Safety.

With the Republicans reeling from these rescues, the Baroness introduces two prominent members of the League of the Scarlet Pimpernel – Sir Andrew Ffoulkes and Lord Antony Dewhurst. Lord Antony explains how 'the Scarlet Pimpernel works in the dark, and his identity is only known under the solemn oath of secrecy to his immediate followers'. When a young French lady (Suzanne de Tournay) is intrigued by the name 'The Scarlet Pimpernel', Sir Andrew's eyes 'shone with enthusiasm; hero-worship, love, admiration for his leader seemed literally to glow upon his face. "The Scarlet Pimpernel, Mademoiselle," he said at last, "is the name of a humble English wayside flower; but it is also the name chosen to hide the identity of the best and bravest man in all the world."'

It transpires that Sir Percy Blakeney, one of the wealthiest men in England, is married to Marguerite Saint-Just, said to be just about the most beautiful and intelligent woman in the whole of Europe. She is described as being 'tall...with magnificent presence and regal figure' and a 'sweet, almost childlike mouth, straight chiselled nose, round chin and delicate throat'. She has a penchant for wearing large hats with huge plumes which 'threw a shadow across the classic brow with the aureole of auburn hair'. But for all her style, Marguerite is perceived as a traitor for having betrayed the Marquis de Saint-Cyr and his family to the guillotine. Consequently Sir Percy, who loves Marguerite deeply but hates what she did, shows no love for her,

The Pimpernel's arch enemy, the cunning Chauvelin (Martin Shaw).

preferring to play the fool. In turn, Marguerite, although she once loved him, now sees him as vain and pompous. And of course she has no idea that her husband is really the Scarlet Pimpernel.

The Baroness visualises Sir Percy as 'tall...even for an Englishman, broad-shouldered and massively-built, he would have been called unusually good-looking, but for a certain lazy expression in his deep-set blue eyes, and that perpetually inane laugh which seemed to disfigure his strong, clearly-cut mouth'. Everyone in England accepts that he is stupid, partly because generations of Blakeneys have been notoriously dull and also because his mother died insane. In short, it is the perfect disguise.

To destroy the League of the Scarlet Pimpernel and capture its leader, the worried French authorities send agent Chauvelin to England. Chauvelin, 'a clever, shrewd-looking personality, with a curious fox-like expression in the deep, sunken eyes', approaches Marguerite for help on account of their past association. She turns him down but when he acquires incriminating evidence against her brother Armand, a League member, she is forced to assist in order to save Armand from prosecution.

Meanwhile the foppish Sir Percy comes up with a little rhyme which does the society rounds:

'We seek him here, we seek him there,
Those Frenchies seek him everywhere.
Is he in heaven? – Is he in hell?
That demmed, elusive Pimpernel?'

Backed into a corner over her brother, Marguerite steals a scrap of paper from Sir Andrew Ffoulkes at Lord Grenville's ball. It reveals details of a meeting of the League leaders. She hands the paper to Chauvelin who, hiding himself in a room, cleverly deduces that Sir Percy is the leader. Horrified at what she has done, Marguerite tells Sir Percy about Chauvelin and her brother. Sir Percy promises to help Armand and sails for France. In his absence, Marguerite goes through his room and stumbles across a ring bearing an engraving of a scarlet pimpernel.

Realising that Sir Percy is the Pimpernel and that she has therefore unwittingly betrayed her own husband, she enlists Sir Andrew's help. Hurriedly they sail to Calais to warn Sir Percy that Chauvelin knows his secret identity and has laid a trap for him. Although they fail to warn him in time, Sir Percy outsmarts Chauvelin and returns to England unscathed. While the love between him and Marguerite is renewed, Chauvelin is disgraced.

Baroness Orczy was pleased with the result of her labours and began hawking it around publishers. However, her confidence proved misplaced as *The Scarlet Pimpernel* was rejected by no fewer than twelve publishers. Undeterred, she and her husband decided to adapt it as a stage play, and it was accepted by husband-and-wife

The Kinks borrowed Baroness Orczy's famous lines for their 1966 hit 'Dedicated Follower of Fashion' – an appropriate title for the suave Sir Percy.

The Pimpernel and his colleagues frequently operate under cover of darkness.

actor/managers Fred Terry and Julia Neilson – but only after what Julia Neilson described as 'drastic revision' had taken place.

In her book *This for Remembrance*, Julia Neilson wrote: 'Our chief criticism of the original version was that all the exciting events happened "off stage". The audience never saw any of the Pimpernel's wonderful exploits, which were spoken of so freely by the other characters.' To remedy this, Fred Terry and writer Louis Calvert composed an entirely new opening scene in which Sir Percy, disguised as an old hag, rescues the

Comtesse de Tournay and her daughter from the guillotine. Now, argued Neilson, 'the audience had seen the Pimpernel *do* something and so were more ready to accept the heroic feats performed between the acts'.

Attracting the services of the Terrys was a major coup for the Baroness, for they were highly regarded, hailed by one contemporary observer as 'peerless performers in sword and cloak drama'. Indeed when Fred Terry died on 17 April 1933, the *News Chronicle* wrote: 'As an actor he was at his best in romantic and picturesque parts, for which his handsome presence and splendid voice peculiarly suited him. We do not grow actors of his type in these anaemic days, and if they did exist, we have no plays for them.'

The production, written under the pseudonym of 'Orczy-Barstow', opened to a packed house at the Theatre Royal, Nottingham, on 15 October 1903 with Terry as Sir Percy and Neilson as Marguerite. The *Nottingham Daily Guardian* reported enthusiastically: 'It is an interesting and, in many respects, even an absorbing tale which the authors set out to tell, and although the device providing the dilemma on which at one time Lady Blakeney looks like being impaled, is not absolutely unfamiliar, it has furnished the playwrights with abundant inspiration ...The result is a play which Miss Neilson and Mr. Terry should find an eminently acceptable addition to their repertoire.'

The next step was to transfer the play to London, but leading West End producer Frank Curzon was distinctly unimpressed. 'This is all right for the provinces, but it won't do for London,' he told Fred Terry. 'The press will never stand for it.'

'I bet you five pounds it will,' replied Terry.

'I bet you fifty it won't,' retorted Curzon.

The Scarlet Pimpernel eventually made it to the West End, at the New Theatre (now the Albery) on 5 January 1905. Curzon's fears were not unfounded. The critics slated it. 'I sat for three mortal hours trying in vain to find something to praise,' wrote *The Times* while the *Daily Mail* added ominously: 'The Scarlet Pimpernel is a plant which blooms at morn and dies at night. This will be the fate of the play named after it.'

Despite these gloomy predictions, Fred Terry had the last laugh. The play was an immediate success with the public and went on to run for years in London, breaking many records in the process. In total, Terry played the Pimpernel 3,000 times – and after each hundredth performance, he sent a copy of the scathing review to the management of the *Daily Mail*. The most dramatic performance occurred at the Strand Theatre on 13 October 1915 when the play was interrupted by a zeppelin raid which killed thirty-eight people and left a further eighty-seven injured. Terry marched on stage and asked the audience whether they wanted the show to continue. They roared their approval and burst into a chorus of 'God Save the King'.

As the Baroness had hoped, the success of the stage play stimulated renewed interest in her novel and *The Scarlet Pimpernel* was published by Greening & Co., Ltd on 12 January 1905, dedicated to Julia Neilson and Fred Terry 'whose genius created the roles of Sir Percy and Lady Blakeney on the stage'. Unlike the play, the novel was well received, not least by the then Home Secretary, Sir William Joynson-Hicks, who told the author: 'You have put your finger on what is best and truest in the English character.' The Baroness was flattered that Sir Percy was considered so authentic and later wrote: 'that was what I aimed at when I first conceived him: a perfect presentation of an English gentleman'.

Although she had always had faith in her creation, Baroness Orczy was taken aback by the success of the novel and the demand for sequels. She went on to revive Sir Percy in *I Will Repay* (1906), *The Elusive Pimpernel* (1908), *Eldorado* (1913), *Lord Tony's Wife* (1917), *The League of the Scarlet Pimpernel* (1919), *The First Sir Percy* (1920) (set in Holland), *The Triumph of the Scarlet Pimpernel* (1922), *Pimpernel and Rosemary* (1924) (set in Hungary), *Sir Percy Hits Back* (1927), *Adventures of the Scarlet Pimpernel* (1929), *The Way of the Scarlet Pimpernel* (1933), *Sir Percy Leads the Band* (1936) and *Mam'zelle Guillotine* (1940). Additionally, Sir Percy appears as the storyteller in her 1932 novel, *A Child of the Revolution*. None of these works, however, was able to recapture the popularity of the original.

Although the various Scarlet Pimpernel-related adventures are her best-known writings, the Baroness penned a total of sixty-eight published volumes. Whilst historical romance was her forte, *The Old Man in the Corner* stories showed that she was no slouch with detective fiction and, in 1910, she created another new detective character in *Lady Molly of Scotland Yard*. Like the author, Lady Molly de Mazareen was a titled lady although there is doubt as to how authentic Lady Molly's title is. The Baroness writes: 'Some say she is the daughter of a duke, others that she was born in the gutter and that the handle has been soldered on to her name in order to give her style and influence.' Lady Molly solves twelve cases – mystery adventures as well as more traditional crimes – which have baffled the finest brains at Scotland Yard until she steps in. Her methods sometimes appear unprofessional to her male colleagues but her impressive results earn their admiration. Each case is narrated by a female assistant who offers a précis of the crime before Lady Molly makes her bow. In keeping with the times, the stories are mildly feminist in attitude but have been dismissed as overwritten and sentimental. They did little to enhance Baroness Orczy's literary reputation.

She featured similar cases in *Skin o' My Tooth*, a 1928 collection of stories featuring Patrick Mulligan, an Irish lawyer practising in England, but was on safer ground when reverting to historical adventure with *The Man in Grey* (1918) and *Castles in the Air* (1922). The former chronicles the triumph of Napoleonic secret agent Fernand against members of the Chouans in 1809, while *Castles in the Air* features seven cases of M. Hector Ratichon, an unscrupulous volunteer police agent in Paris in

1813. The Baroness was back in the country and period of history of her greatest triumph.

In 1918 she and her husband moved to Monte Carlo and took up residence at the Villa Bijou. Intense, witty and darkly attractive, Baroness Orczy became a welcome guest at the highest courts of Europe. Laden with jewellery, she wore rich, low-cut gowns usually topped with a big hat, decorated with a huge ostrich feather – uncannily like the one Marguerite wore in *The Scarlet Pimpernel*. The only thing to which she ever took exception at these society parties was being addressed as 'Baroness Pimpernel'.

Shortly after her son had written a biography of the Scarlet Pimpernel, entitled *The Gay Adventurer*, under the pseudonym 'John Blakeney', the Second World War broke out. Although her permanent home was in Monte Carlo, the outbreak of war found Baroness Orczy in London but, even at the age of seventy-four, she possessed enough energy to hurry back to Monte Carlo and carry out relief work among her neighbours. Then, when the Germans invaded France, she and her husband were trapped in Monte Carlo, terrified to speak English because they lived next door to the local Gestapo headquarters.

Her beloved Montagu died there in 1943 and her faithful maid, who had contributed many years of devoted service, was arrested by the Italians. Despite the Baroness's repeated efforts, she was unable to secure her release. Just before the town was liberated, Baroness Orczy's villa was bombed by the RAF and she returned to England to spend her last years in a secluded country house at Henley-on-Thames. She died at the age of eighty-two, on 12 November 1947 – the same year in which her autobiography was published.

Marguerite Blakeney and Baroness Orczy shared a similar taste in hats.

In tribute, the *New York Herald Tribune* said that she had 'a natural gift for swift narration, a vivid imagination and an appropriately flamboyant style'. *The Times* of London was more grudging in its praise. 'She could hardly be classed as a serious student of history or a writer of outstanding originality,' it wrote. 'The idea of her celebrated book is of a simple and naïve romantic ingenuity, and while the form and the writing cannot claim any conspicuous literary merit, the straightforward narrative hit the taste of a large reading public.' The obituary concluded that both she and the Pimpernel 'nevertheless both became household names for a grateful multitude'.

CHAPTER THREE

SIR PERCY ON STAGE AND SCREEN

As a master of disguise, a character capable of blending in with any background, it is only natural that the Scarlet Pimpernel has been equally at home on film, television, radio and stage as he was in books. To date, there have been at least seventeen different productions based on Baroness Orczy's immortal character.

Given the success of the Terrys' London stage version, it was only a matter of time before the blossoming movie industry decreed the Pimpernel worthy of celluloid treatment, and in 1917 American silent star Dustin Farnum, best known for cowboy roles in *The Squaw Man* and *The Virginian*, became the first screen Sir Percy in *The Scarlet Pimpernel*. The film stirred up a veritable hornets' nest as Baroness Orczy, encouraged by her husband, took Fred Terry and Julia Neilson to court in a dispute over the film rights. The Baroness claimed that she had retained the rights to produce *The Scarlet Pimpernel* as a cinema film and had only given the Terrys the rights to produce the play on stage in their lifetimes. But when the case went to court in June 1924, the Chancery Division ruled that the Terrys had the film rights as well as the stage rights.

It dawned on the Baroness that she had given away the rights to her creation too quickly and too cheaply: it is rumoured that she sold them to the Terrys for just £200, although Julia Neilson claimed that she and Fred Terry paid the Baroness £20,000 in royalties over the years. Given the general air of confusion, it was little surprise that another legal wrangle accompanied the release in 1928 of the second silent film – *The Triumph of the Scarlet Pimpernel*, starring Scottish/Canadian matinée idol Matheson Lang. This time it was agreed that the Terrys had the rights to *The Scarlet Pimpernel* but that it should be made clear that the film had absolutely no connection with the

Leslie Howard brought the Scarlet Pimpernel to life in Alexander Korda's 1934 film.

Production of the Korda film was sometimes a fraught affair with the director fired after the first day of filming.

long-running stage play. It was a mess, further complicated when the Terrys sold some of the film rights.

Although the play enhanced the Baroness's reputation, there is little doubt that she felt she had been taken advantage of. But of course she had never expected *The Scarlet Pimpernel* to be such a success. It is alleged that such was her anger when the play originally took off and she realised she wasn't earning as much from it as she had hoped, that she made one crucial change to the manuscript of her novel before re-submitting it to publishers. That was to reveal Sir Percy's age as being 'a year or two on the right side of thirty', supposedly to infuriate Fred Terry who was forty when he first played the part.

Meanwhile the Terrys' stage play continued to draw widespread acclaim and was translated into numerous foreign languages for overseas productions. On 14 May 1928, a special matinée performance was given at the Palace Theatre, London, in the presence of King George V and Queen Mary, with all proceeds going to the King George Pension Fund for Actors and Actresses. The king is said to have told Fred Terry that he enjoyed the play as much as ever.

Age was no bar to Terry's swashbuckling and, on Boxing Day 1928, at sixty-five years old, he revived *The Scarlet Pimpernel* for the Christmas season at the Strand Theatre. This time the critics were kinder. '*The Scarlet Pimpernel* wears well,' wrote the *Daily Telegraph*. 'It has all the elements calculated to raise the emotions.' And *The Times* called it 'a play that has many of the marks of time and yet has plenty of life in it'.

Shortly before Fred Terry's death, Hungarian producer Alexander Korda acquired the movie rights and began filming a star-studded version of *The Scarlet Pimpernel*. Leslie Howard played Sir Percy with Merle Oberon as Marguerite and Raymond Massey as the dastardly Chauvelin. Although of Hungarian descent, Howard was seen as the quintessential Englishman whose indifference made him irresistible to women. He was therefore supremely cast as Sir Percy and his screen romance with the beautiful Merle Oberon was mirrored in their real-life affair. Oberon subsequently married Alexander Korda. The production got off to a shaky start when Korda fired director Rowland Brown after the first day's filming, replacing him with Harold Young. But when it was released in December

Leslie Howard and Merle Oberon as Sir Percy and Marguerite.

1934, the film did good business, grossing £420,000 despite some cinema-goers expressing disgust at Miss Oberon's display of cleavage.

Three years later to the month saw the release of *The Return of the Scarlet Pimpernel*, produced by Korda and directed by Hans Schwarz. It starred British stage actor Barry K. Barnes as Sir Percy and the cast also featured a young James Mason, but the film failed to match the box-office appeal of the original.

Leslie Howard returned to the basic concept of the Scarlet Pimpernel character for a 1941 film, *Pimpernel Smith*, which he produced, directed and starred in. Giving the Pimpernel story a modern slant, Howard played a professor of archaeology who went into war-torn Europe to rescue refugees.

In the meantime, the stage play had been revived at the Q Theatre in Kew over Christmas 1936 with Donald Wolfit as Sir Percy and his wife Rosalind Iden as Marguerite. Two years later, over Christmas 1938, the play re-surfaced again, this time at the Embassy Theatre with Derrick de Marney and Dorothy Dickson as the Blakeneys and Esme Percy as a much-praised Chauvelin.

The year 1950 was a big one for Baroness Orczy's hero. February 5th saw the transmission of the first television adaptation when the BBC broadcast a 110-minute version of *The Scarlet Pimpernel.* Produced by Fred O'Donovan and adapted from the stage play, it starred James Carney as Sir Percy and Margaretta Scott as Lady Marguerite Blakeney. The same cast repeated the performance on 14 January 1951, those being the days when repeats invariably necessitated doing the whole thing over again.

Also in 1950, Alexander Korda hired film-makers Michael Powell and Emeric Pressburger to make *The Elusive Pimpernel.* Korda cast David Niven as Sir Percy as part of a deal with producer Sam Goldwyn who had Niven under contract. However, because he was in dispute with Goldwyn, Niven refused to turn up for the first day of shooting and all the location work had to be done with doubles. Margaret Leighton played Marguerite and the line-up also included Cyril Cusack and Jack Hawkins.

Raymond Massey looking suitably devilish as Chauvelin in the 1934 film version of The Scarlet Pimpernel.

Niven's contract was just one of the problems which beset the film. Pressburger found writing the screenplay such heavy going that, in despair, he went to see his fellow Hungarian, Korda. In his biography, Pressburger is quoted as saying: 'I went to see Alex one day and cursed both the Baroness and her books. I told him I could not do it, I could not write a script from this. And Alex looked at me very seriously, almost hurt, and said: "But my dear Imre, how can you say that? She was a Hungarian."'

Perhaps sensing the need for desperate measures, Korda concocted an elaborate publicity stunt in which he claimed that atomic energy rays had destroyed 20,000 feet of film in transit from location to the studios. Maybe it was just wishful thinking, since the movie opened on 3 November 1950 to bad reviews and worse business. The *Daily Express* set the tone: 'Niven plays the Scarlet Pimpernel with the sheepish lack of enthusiasm of a tone deaf man called upon to sing solo in church. His companions lumber through their parts like schoolboys about to go down with mumps.' *The Times* described Niven as 'looking less like Sir Percy Blakeney than the

A guillotine scene from Korda's version of The Scarlet Pimpernel.

dame in some nightmare pantomime', while *Punch* magazine added: 'I never thought I should feel inclined to leave a Powell and Pressburger film before the end; but I did here.'

According to Pressburger, the Americans disliked the title *The Elusive Pimpernel* because they thought it was some terrible skin disease. So it was eventually released in the United States in 1955 as *The Fighting Pimpernel.*

While the big-budget films attracted the attention, the Scarlet Pimpernel was also making a name for himself on radio. Marius Goring played Sir Percy in a six-part series for the BBC in 1949 and, from 1 December 1952, starred in *The New Adventures of the Scarlet Pimpernel* on Radio Luxemburg. Two years later, he recorded 52 radio adventures for NBC radio. And it was Goring who co-produced and starred in the next TV version, produced by Towers of London and screened on the new ITV channel in 1956. Eighteen thirty-minute episodes were made, with the emphasis very much on the Pimpernel's amazing power of disguise. One moment Goring would appear as an old woman, the next as a barrow boy. Stanley van Beers played Chauvelin with future Doctor Who Patrick Troughton as Sir Andrew Ffoulkes. Minor roles were taken by

Christopher Lee, John Laurie (who went on to play Fraser in *Dad's Army*) and Peter O'Toole (as a soldier). And Esme Percy, who had appeared as Chauvelin in the 1938 stage version, cropped up as a blind man in one episode. Being an action adventure series in the mould of ITV's other early efforts – *The Adventures of Robin Hood*, *The Adventures of William Tell*, *The Buccaneers*, *Ivanhoe* and *The Count of Monte Cristo*, to name but a few – the love story element was relegated to the extent that the character of Marguerite scarcely featured.

In 1966 the Scarlet Pimpernel received the *Carry On* treatment, although the film was simply titled *Don't Lose Your Head* (without the familiar *Carry On* prefix) because of a dispute between the new distributors, Rank, and the previous distributors, Anglo-Amalgamated. The inimitable Sid James played Sir Rodney Ffing (pronounced Effing), alias the daring Black Fingernail. The Chauvelin role went to Kenneth Williams as Citizen Camembert while Peter Gilmore (who later starred in *The Onedin Line*) appeared as Robespierre. Other character names were suitably Gallic, including the Duc de Pommefrit (Charles Hawtrey) and Citizen Bidet (Peter Butterworth). Talbot Rothwell, who wrote most of the *Carry On* films, said at the time: 'This is Sid James as Errol Flynn. It's like one of those swashbuckling romps that were made throughout the 1930s and 1940s, but instead of Flynn there's Sid, and instead of Basil Rathbone

The Paris mob storm through the streets in a scene from the 1937 film The Return of the Scarlet Pimpernel.

there's Kenneth Williams. The only real difference is that this is deliberately funny whereas the originals were never directly humorous. And it's probably the only time you'll ever get to see Sid James in a dress!'

Apparently James was none too enamoured at having to play in drag, particularly when the crew started chatting him up and Kenneth Williams proposed marriage! In the end, he hid in his dressing-room, smoking his pipe. James proved himself an adept swordsman on this film and even managed to sneak an ad-lib into the final version – a rarity in *Carry On*, where the scripts were considered sacrosanct. It occurred when Charles Hawtrey's Duc de Pommefrit was waiting on the executioner's block. James suggested that someone should bring Hawtrey a note and he would toss it in the basket in front of the block, saying he would read it later...

Top: Barry K. Barnes as Sir Percy in The Return of the Scarlet Pimpernel.

Inset: A young James Mason in the same film.

The merriment was lost on Kenneth Williams, whose diary entry for 16 December 1973 read: 'There was nothing but rubbish on the television. Old films including *Don't Lose Your Head*...I was as bad as ever, all posh voice and sneers and convincing no one.'

From 20 April 1969, the BBC screened a new ten-part television series, *The Elusive*

Jim Dale as Lord Darcy and Sid James as Sir Rodney Ffing (pronounced Effing) in the Carry On comedy Don't Lose Your Head.

Pimpernel, starring Anton Rodgers as Sir Percy Blakeney. Transmitted in the Sunday tea-time slot which was then reserved for dramatisations of classic novels, it co-starred Bernard Hepton as Chauvelin, Diane Fletcher as Marguerite and Roy Marsden as Sir Andrew Ffoulkes and was adapted by John Hawkesworth from two of Baroness Orczy's novels – *The Elusive Pimpernel* and *Eldorado*. Campbell Logan produced and Gerald Blake directed.

Billed as a 'classic adventure of passion, honour and intrigue', *The Scarlet Pimpernel* resurfaced in 1982 in a made-for-TV film starring the inevitable Jane Seymour (as Marguerite), Anthony Andrews (as Sir Percy) and Ian McKellen as Chauvelin. Directed by Clive Donner, it was, at 150 minutes, almost twice as long as the Leslie Howard original and, to some critics, seemed it.

The early 1980s saw renewed interest in the Pimpernel. Novelist C. Guy Clayton recounted Marguerite's solo adventures in three volumes of *The Blakeney Papers* and, after a lengthy absence from the stage, the play returned to the West End in 1985.

Starring as Sir Percy at Her Majesty's Theatre was Donald Sinden in a production by Nicholas Hytner, who subsequently directed *The Madness of King George.*

Sir Donald Sinden recalls a gift from John Cabot, who had been one of the juveniles in Fred Terry's company. 'John was kind enough to present me with Fred Terry's snuff-box. But I was puzzled by its small size. According to John, all actors in those days would carry a small emergency snuff-box in case stage management forgot to put the real bigger box on the set. John then asked me if I was playing the Old Woman at the beginning of the show. Apparently Fred was initially happy to put on the disguise until somebody pointed out that nobody knew it was him acting so convincingly. So he hired an old actress to play the part without a credit. Audiences would then whisper to each other in amazement about the brilliance of Fred's performance!'

Kenneth Williams flared his nostrils to good effect as Citizen Camembert in Don't Lose Your Head.

On the first night at Chichester, before transferring to the West End, Sinden wielded Fred Terry's spy-glass and wore his jabot – the lace frills on his shirt. He also offered an additional touch of his own.

'For the scene at the Lion d'Or – not a very select establishment – the audience sees Brogard, the disgusting landlord, take several dead rats (in reality, plastic ones filled with spaghetti) and squeeze their insides into the soup he serves to Chauvelin. A barrister friend saw the show and came backstage afterwards and quipped, referring to the scene, that it must have been ratatouille. I thought that it was such a good line that I put in the show and it got the biggest laugh of the evening.'

In 1997 it was the turn of the musical version of *The Scarlet Pimpernel.* It is believed that impresario Sir Bernard Delfont had once planned to cast Bruce Forsyth as Sir Percy in a Pimpernel musical but the project never materialised. However, the Broadway production (starring Douglas Sills as Sir Percy, Christine Andreas as Marguerite and Terrence Mann as Chauvelin) has proved more successful, already earning a clutch of Tony award nominations. The musical concentrates on the love story and features songs with titles such as 'Pimpernel Fanfare' and 'Madame Guillotine'. Baroness Orczy really did have no idea what she had created all those years ago.

CHAPTER FOUR

THE ADAPTABLE PIMPERNEL

The trail of this latest adaptation of *The Scarlet Pimpernel* dates back to 1931 when distinguished Hungarian producer/director Alexander Korda bought the rights to the book. Three years later, Korda's production company, London Films, made the movie starring Leslie Howard and it proved so successful that, unlike the Baroness or the Terrys, they decided to keep the rights.

Julian Murphy, producer of the 1998 films, explains: 'London Films still own the rights and about eight years ago they brought the idea of doing a new television version of *The Scarlet Pimpernel to* the BBC. Scripts were done but, as is often the case with such big productions, the moment never quite came when the money and will met to make it all happen. When I arrived at the BBC's Pebble Mill, Birmingham, studios in 1996, this was one of the projects on the development slate there. To be honest, it wasn't a very live project – it was just hanging around – because such a massive undertaking as this was not something which the BBC could afford to do alone.

'Anyway, the decision was taken by London Films and the BBC to redevelop the scripts and take *The Scarlet Pimpernel* in a new direction. The scripts which had been written were very faithful to the books and were done as hours rather than the 95-minute films we have now. And it's very hard to do a book in an hour. So we approached Richard Carpenter whose work we knew through series such as *Robin of Sherwood*. My feeling was that for *The Scarlet Pimpernel to* work, it needed a thorough overhaul and updating. I didn't think that the Pimpernel that thrilled audiences in the 1930s would necessarily work now, although the basic characters and the mystery behind them are still wonderful. Baroness Orczy's books weren't classic novels like *Pride and Prejudice,* where to change a word would amount to sacrilege, so we decided to make alterations. Richard Carpenter is a master of giving a modern spin to history and was therefore the obvious choice as writer.'

Julian Murphy, producer of the 1998 films, on set with Martin Shaw who plays Chauvelin.

Richard Carpenter is a man with a pedigree of historical adventure. Starting

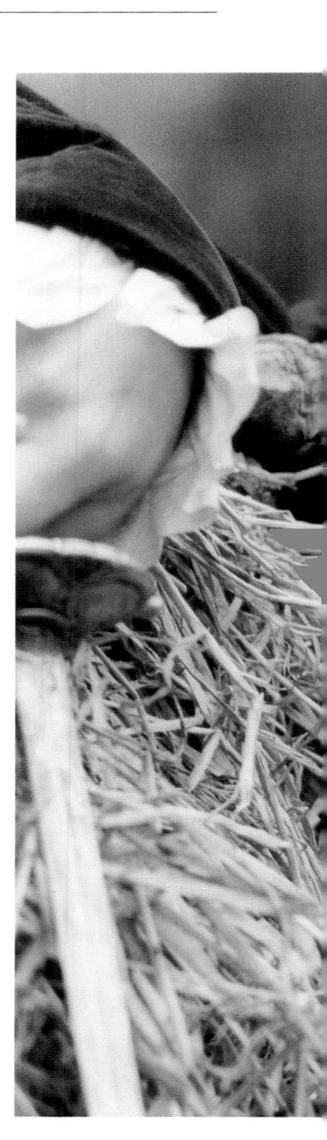

training as an actor at the Old Vic in 1956, he went on to appear in the West End, in ten feature films and over 200 television productions, most notably as Peter Parker in the 1959 ITV action adventure series *Knight Errant*, a show which gave early breaks to Oliver Reed, David McCallum and *Coronation Street*'s William Roache (a.k.a. Ken Barlow). It was while working on *Knight Errant* that Richard began learning to write for TV, a trade he put to good use for the first time with the popular 26-part children's series *Catweazle*, for which he won the Writers' Guild Award. He repeated the feat the following year for his scripts for another successful series, *The Adventures of Black Beauty*.

He went on to create and write two series of *Dick Turpin* (starring Richard O'Sullivan) and, from 1983, three series of the hugely successful *Robin of Sherwood*. His dramatisation of Mary Norton's *The Borrowers* (which starred Ian Holm and Penelope Wilton) helped that series win the BAFTA Award for Best Children's Drama. His prolific output has also included the cartoon series *Doctor Snuggles, The Winjin Pom,* produced by Spitting Image, the four-part children's drama *Stanley's Dragon* and two series of *Out of Sight* for which he again won the Writers' Guild Award for Best Children's Drama.

He recalls: 'I first got involved with *The Scarlet Pimpernel* when my agent heard that producer Julian Murphy was looking for a writer – "someone like the guy who did *Robin of Sherwood*". I said I'd love to do it, but I didn't think it would be possible because at the time I was working on the second series of *Out of Sight*. But I went to a meeting and reckoned I could do both.

'I already had a good general idea of the character of Sir Percy. I had read the first Scarlet Pimpernel book, albeit a long time ago, and I remembered the Leslie Howard film. I was given a lot of research material, but I was particularly keen to find out more about the French Revolution. Fortunately a *Chronicle of the French Revolution* was published to mark the 200th anniversary and that proved invaluable, along with various other history books. Discovering the social history of the period was important to provide me with an authentic background for the stories. I needed to know things like whether they had cabs in Paris, who had baths, all manner of daily minutiae.

'In the course of my research, I learned a great deal about the French Revolution. There were so many wonderful characters. For example, there was a dragoon officer

The character of Henri (James Callis) is based on a real rebel aristocrat from the Revolution.

who was awarded all kinds of medals and prizes for bravery, but he did like to wear ladies' clothes all the time and it brought him into a certain amount of disrepute because there weren't many cross-dressers in those days. I just thought, what a wonderful character for a climax to one of the films, with Percy fighting a duel with him in full eighteenth-century drag, which is obviously much more over the top. In the end, I swapped it around and we had a woman dressed as a man. That's what I love about the story – those details. Another real character I was able to incorporate was Monsieur Henri, the young rebel aristocrat from the Vendée, in the second film.

'I think you have to go for comedy with the Pimpernel otherwise it can become very po-faced and the audience won't accept it. I had to lose a wonderful scene where two old biddies are scrubbing the floor and one of them farts and the other says: "Christ,

Hortense, what did you have for supper last night?" Then we pan up and we see they're scrubbing the blood from the steps of the guillotine. Unfortunately it's those scenes that go when you're cutting the scripts to length because they're not essential to the plot. It's a shame because often they're the scenes that people remember, rather than the story.

'On re-reading Baroness Orczy's novels, I had to say: "Forget the books, but keep the basic character." As a result, the first film is based loosely on *The Scarlet Pimpernel* and *The Elusive Pimpernel* while the second and third scripts are my own creations, although the Baroness herself did write a book about Percy rescuing the Dauphin, which forms the basic plot for the third film. I must admit that the books are a bit old-fashioned now – very Mills & Boon – but the character of Sir Percy is immortal. Baroness Orczy was a genius in creating this amazing dual-identity personality who in turn has spawned other dual-identity heroes like Superman, Batman and Zorro. It's a classic: the mild-mannered little man who at night becomes someone else. James Bond is the same – he uses the front of being an international gambler and womaniser – but the Scarlet Pimpernel was certainly one of the first. There's something fascinating about a dual identity. Sir Percy Blakeney is this amiable aristocrat who is a sort of chinless wonder, an eighteenth-century Hooray Henry – quite witty but fairly ineffectual, you imagine. Then he goes off and does these brave and daring deeds. Why Blakeney can't tell anyone he's the Scarlet Pimpernel is beyond me! But it's a literary device and I suppose readers put themselves in the hero's situation. It's the purest escapism.

'The important points to remember for whoever plays the Pimpernel are: he has to have the natural arrogance of an aristocrat who is used to having servants doing everything for him; he has to have enormous charm; he's got to be able to do the "silly ass" part, which is very much a traditional character in English dramatic fiction; and you also have to believe that he's as tough as nails. All in all, it's not an easy part to play, but the court jester facet is the most important. Also there is the extraordinary relationship with Marguerite which is resolved at the end of the first book. But the big problem is that, once your James Bond character is married, you lose something because he's not a dashing hero any more – he's a married man with a mortgage and he's not available. The director, Patrick Lau, helped me a great deal with this. He said that it was a marriage based on a strong sexual attraction (Percy and Marguerite can't wait to rip each other's clothes off) but at the same time they have, on the surface, quite a prickly relationship. She's very much an independent woman because she's French, she's had a very hard life and she was a successful actress as well as a Republican. He's an aristocrat with a pedigree going back to the Norman conquest but he too is very strong-willed. In 1790 for an Englishman to marry a French Republican actress was very daring because in those days an actress was one up from a tart. And that shows that Percy doesn't give a damn.'

At the core of the Pimpernel story is the passionate, volatile relationship between Sir Percy and his wife Marguerite.

Whilst remaining faithful to the three principals, Richard Carpenter has injected a little extra spice into the relationship between Marguerite and Chauvelin. 'Baroness Orczy depicts Chauvelin as a rather desiccated sixty-year-old,' he says. 'She refers to him constantly as a spider, but I have made him younger and, to tighten the tension a little, I've made him Marguerite's lover before she met Percy. After all, it's in the book that she had known Chauvelin before so why not make them lovers? It strengthens the triangle between the three because it's an irritant to Percy to know that his wife has been with this other man in the past. That is an ongoing feeling which serves to make Percy and Chauvelin professional and personal antagonists. In fact, I'm surprised Orczy didn't think of it because it's in the tradition of a romantic novel.

'Interestingly, Raymond Massey played Chauvelin quite young – and quite handsome – in the Leslie Howard film, but he didn't really get hold of the part. It's probably Leslie Howard's best performance, which is lucky because everyone else in that film is terrible. Everything about the film has dated horribly apart from Howard's performance which is as fresh as a daisy. You just never take your eyes off him. He played the Pimpernel with a lot of humour and enormous style.'

Richard Carpenter has also endeavoured to present a more balanced view of the French Revolution than Baroness Orczy did. 'She clearly studied the French Revolution,' he says, 'but she had a very blinkered view of it. She was a first-class snob and very right-wing and that was how she saw the Revolution – through the eyes of an extreme right-winger.

'There is one passage in *The Scarlet Pimpernel* novel where Percy disguises himself as "a repulsive old Jew" and Orczy's tone is strongly anti-semitic and extremely offensive, implying that all Jews are thieving and nasty. Obviously that had to be rewritten.

'As an aristocrat herself, perhaps it was inevitable that she would side throughout with the aristocracy. From her writing, she obviously thought that all aristocrats were noble and went to the guillotine with stiff upper lips whereas she considered all Republicans to be blood-thirsty maniacs. I've tried to redress the balance and, to that end, I've made Percy humanitarian, rather than political. As I see it, his aim is to rescue anyone from the guillotine – not just the aristocracy.

'As well as attempting to show both sides of the French Revolution, I've tried to relate key real-life incidents to the plot of *The Scarlet Pimpernel*. I think we've gone far more deeply into the Revolution than the Baroness did – without turning the films into documentaries – and we've tried to bring the story into the twentieth century. I don't think a modern audience will have any difficulty relating to the stories because I think people will see a James Bond-type character from an earlier age.

'Many think the French Revolution was all about the people kicking out the aristocrats and that was that. But in fact it was part of a bitter civil war. The Royalists

Among his many attributes, Sir Percy is an accomplished swordsman.

Another nobleman prepares to meet his fate, watched by a bloodthirsty crowd.

used to nail the Republicans to barn doors, while the Republicans favoured what came to be known as a "Republican Wedding". They would tie their victims together in bundles on barges and sink them in the River Loire. So both sides were capable of extreme cruelty, and something like 250,000 people died – Danton used the word "holocaust". In the final episode, Chauvelin warns that the people who made the Revolution will be destroyed by it and of course they were. They all fought among themselves for power – Marat was killed in his bath by Charlotte Corday, Danton was killed on a trumped-up charge by Robespierre and then finally the Assembly had had enough of Robespierre and had him beheaded. There are parallels with what happened to the chief of the secret police in Russia. He had a huge office on the top floor of the

KGB building and three men turned up with guns, took him to the basement and shot him. It's rather like the difference between Karl Marx and Stalin – the men who proposed the French Revolution were great philosophers and political thinkers like Rousseau and Voltaire, but as always happens in revolution, it swings to totalitarianism and you end up with people like Robespierre running the show. I had a wonderful picture of Robespierre with hundreds of guillotines ... and he's guillotining the executioner because there's nobody else left! I've tried to show how, in a sense, the mob ran Robespierre. He justified what he did by saying it was the "will of the people" and he always insisted publicly that he was on their side, yet in truth he was terrified of the people.

'Studying the period has certainly been an education for me. It's amazing to think that as well as the internal revolution, France was tackling England, Austria, Spain,

Sir Percy's engaging smile hides the mind of a ruthless assassin.

At society events such as the Carlton House ball, Sir Percy adopts his most ingenious disguise – that of buffoon.

Belgium and Holland, all of whom declared war on the French. But Napoleon rose from it, France came through and conquered most of Europe within twelve years. It's incredible. No wonder the French look back on it as a glorious episode in their history.'

During his extensive research, Richard felt he got to know the Baroness quite well. 'Then I heard a tape of her talking about the Pimpernel and she sounded frightfully Kensington, which surprised me. When you study someone's work, you feel you know them because they reveal themselves in all sorts of ways. When I did *The Famous Five* in the 1970s, I sat down and read twenty-six Enid Blyton books on the trot. It was an effort because she's only got four basic plots. She had a thing about washing your hands; she had a thing about tunnels; she had a thing about snakes; and a thing about swarthy foreigners. But Enid Blyton had this wonderful story-telling ability which compels you even as an adult. And I got to know her literary devices. For instance whenever she was in a jam, the Famous Five would roll back the carpet and, lo and behold, there'd be a trapdoor leading down to a secret smugglers' cave!

'Similarly, I got to know Baroness Orczy. One of the first things I realised was that she put herself into the books as Marguerite, the very beautiful French actress. Percy was obviously the sort of man the Baroness would have liked to have gone to bed with because she's always talking about his "manly frame" and his rippling muscles. There are no actual sex scenes in the books because in those days you couldn't go much further than describing his physique, but there's a passionate romanticism about the scenes. *The Scarlet Pimpernel* book is written in high romantic form but it works because she has such conviction. She wants to be Marguerite and she's madly in love with Percy and she writes it from Marguerite's point of view.

'It's called "Peggy Sue" writing where people (especially amateur writers) project themselves subconsciously. I get a lot of stuff from Robin Hood fans where you have a new female character who Robin falls in love with and who represents the writer.

'Although I describe Baroness Orczy as in a sense a Mills & Boon writer, you could say the same about the Brontës or Jane Austen. All of their books were very romantic and they all have an enigmatic, saturnine hero – be it Rochester, Darcy or Heathcliff. They're all Byronic figures and Byron was the template for those characters because his exploits were common knowledge.

'Like Enid Blyton – and indeed a lot of popular writers – Orczy has only a limited number of plots. With the Pimpernel books, she has three which she keeps reworking. One plot has Percy in disguise and you don't know it's him until half-way through; another scenario sees Marguerite captured and rescued by Percy; and the third is a family situation, seemingly nothing to do with the Pimpernel at all, until the narrative eventually reaches the period of the French Revolution. Her plots do creak: she doesn't worry about the mechanics of the piece and she doesn't go into much detail. She'll just write things like, "Percy made his escape under cover of darkness." It's up to the reader – or in my case the dramatist – to work out exactly how he did make his escape.

Baroness Orczy saw herself as Marguerite.

'But putting myself into Baroness Orczy's shoes has been great fun and has thrown up all manner of puzzles for me to solve. For example, in the third film I was trying to work out how Percy could follow a particular woman. In the end, I had him buying a cab and becoming a cab driver so that the woman would have to tell him where she wanted to go. You have to come up with inventive ideas like that to do justice to the original. It's all part of the enduring appeal of The Scarlet Pimpernel.'

'Richard has done a tremendous job,' says executive producer Tony Virgo. 'When I arrived as head of drama at Pebble Mill, I was very excited about the prospect of remaking *The Scarlet Pimpernel*, but I didn't like the scripts which were around at the time. They weren't quite a family adventure – more a typical sturdy BBC drama serial. But once we'd got Richard on board, everything changed. Right from our first lunch, he was so enthusiastic and so knowledgeable about the period and he seemed to know the way forward. And of course he's got the track record.'

Richard Carpenter has managed to weave true events into elements of the Baroness's stories. In the third film, he draws on the real happenings of 1794 when the revolutionaries auctioned all of the dead king and queen's personal effects. 'It was a bizarre state of affairs,' says producer Julian Murphy. 'The French leaders put the valuables on display at Versailles and invited nobles from all the countries they were at war with to come to an auction and bid for the royal effects. It went on for about a year. It was madness, twisted.

'Richard has also taken little episodes and characters from the Baroness's many books and short stories. For example, the character of Mademoiselle Guillotine – Gabrielle Damiens – in the second film comes from the Baroness's final Pimpernel book, *Mam'zelle Guillotine*. And Chauvelin's daughter – indeed the fact that Chauvelin even has a daughter – from film two is lifted from one of Baroness Orczy's short stories.

'The French Revolution was a very complicated period of history and we wanted to make the audience realise that it was a time of turbulence and anarchy without losing sight of who is actually fighting who. As Richard says, it's not a documentary. *The Scarlet Pimpernel* is no more a reflection of eighteenth-century French history than James Bond is of the Cold War. The Baroness didn't write it as a documentary – she wrote it as a romance. It's a great and unusual love story about a husband and wife who are on opposite sides in a war. That was one thing we didn't change from the Baroness's first book – the way in which Marguerite unwittingly betrays Sir Percy. The love angle is as important a part of the story as the action adventure and it is the combination of the two which gives *The Scarlet Pimpernel* that special appeal. It appeals to men and women, young and old because it works on all levels.

'Another reason for the longevity of *The Scarlet Pimpernel* is that we're all fascinated by characters who are given the licence to lead a double life, to appear an idiot to one group of people – a man who doesn't care, who spends too much money and cracks bad jokes – and to be someone humanitarian and wildly different in real life. We'd all love that licence, that secret romantic heroism.

Denise Black as local revolutionary leader Gabrielle Damiens, affectionately known as Mademoiselle Guillotine.

'We have had to inject a level of danger and realism which a modern audience wants – and to get us away from the *Carry On* images of the French Revolution. There is certainly less mincing about in this production than in some of the previous versions. Richard E. Grant plays the Pimpernel with a lot of wit and panache, but has avoided the camp.'

CHAPTER FIVE

THEY SEEK HIM HERE...

With Richard Carpenter in place as writer, the next questions to be asked by producer Julian Murphy and executive producer Tony Virgo were: who will play the Scarlet Pimpernel, where will we film it and who will pay for it? The last question was the first to be addressed and a six-month hunt began to find suitable co-producers to help finance the BBC in the £4 million project.

Tony Virgo admits: 'The BBC couldn't possibly have afforded a remake of *The Scarlet Pimpernel* without co-producers and we have been fortunate enough to come up with three: Arts and Entertainment, the New York cable channel which also put out the BBC's *Pride and Prejudice*; ABC from Australia; and TV3 of New Zealand. Probably the biggest obstacle to overcome was convincing people that a programme about the French Revolution and the guillotine could be family viewing, but all three have been tremendous. Hugh McGowan of ABC was at times as elusive as the Pimpernel but was a great enthusiast and almost handed us £300,000 over the desk, there and then. And Delia Fine, drama executive with A and E, said that *The Scarlet Pimpernel* had always been her favourite book. In fact, she was so keen that she came up with the money within a week. As we talked, it was clear that she had her own views about how the books should be adapted and her notes on Richard's first draft were extremely perceptive. She was very keen on emphasising the romance between Percy and Marguerite and she wanted visual romance as well as the blood and guts. She was also keen that the audience should discover in the first two or three minutes precisely who and what the Pimpernel is, whereas in the book it takes much longer.'

The money raised, the next hurdle to be cleared was where to film eighteenth century Paris. 'We knew we had to go abroad for most of the filming,' says Julian Murphy, 'because everywhere that wasn't English had to be French. Going to Paris was unrealistic financially, too restrictive for filming and anyway Paris is essentially Napoleonic – it changed a lot in the early nineteenth century. The eighteenth-century

Securing Richard E. Grant to play the Scarlet Pimpernel represents a major coup for the BBC.

Director Patrick Lau, continuity supervisor Maggie Lewty and Richard E. Grant take a break between filming.

buildings aren't really there any more. Prague was a possibility for a number of reasons. It's used to doing western films, there's a tremendous talent base there, it looks completely different to our English locations and it's actually used by the French as Paris for shows like *Maigret* and *Les Misérables*. Also there was a good exchange rate from the conversion of sterling to Czech crowns, so it made economic sense too.

'After our first recce there with designer Tim Hutchinson in September 1997, we were convinced that we could make it work. We carried on looking for locations right up until Christmas with Patrick Lau, who has directed the first two films. I'd always wanted to work with Patrick but we had problems with his dates because he was filming the BBC science fiction series *Invasion: Earth*. One of the good things about getting Patrick on board at an early stage was that he was able to have an input into the casting – which I always think is critical – although obviously that was something to which we had already given some thought.'

Patrick Lau, whose directing credits include *Dragon's Reach*, *Doctor Finlay*, *Game, Set and Match*, *Countdown to War*, *Hamish Macbeth*, *The Ambassador* and *Coronation Street*, did indeed play a key role in the casting. He says: 'For the Pimpernel, you need to find an actor who can play both sides of the character's personality – the dashing hero as the Pimpernel and the public persona as Sir Percy. So I thought Richard E. Grant was a very good bet because he's got tremendous style and energy. I am one of the few directors who has ever seen him in the theatre when he first

arrived in London from Africa. I saw him at the Orange Tree in a Restoration play, *Man of Mode*, before he hit the movies.

'I like Richard's work a lot, mainly because he's never boring – always daring. If someone can give you that inner momentum, you have a lot to play with. That makes him ideal for the Pimpernel's recklessness because if you analyse the Pimpernel's actions, he is utterly reckless. He doesn't need to rescue people, does he? Richard is also funny and witty with a lovely voice. For Sir Percy, with his play of words and language, it is important to have someone who has that delicacy with words and delivery – the English wit. Very few people can do it, but Richard can. And he's got the lung power and energy to do the speeches because a lot of *The Scarlet Pimpernel* is like a Restoration comedy. If you haven't got that energy, you break the speeches up every three words, which I hate.

'We cast the Pimpernel first before the others fitted in to complete the chemistry. For me, it's like cooking. With Marguerite, you need a heroine who has guts and glamour. Her own background is quite mysterious. She is French and is supposed to have

Director Patrick Lau (above) played a key role in the casting, particularly that of Elizabeth McGovern (below) as Lady Marguerite Blakeney.

forsaken all her earlier revolutionary leanings to marry an English aristocrat, all for love. I wanted to portray Marguerite and Percy as quite a fiery couple who always row in public. I had seen Elizabeth McGovern in the theatre, playing *The Misanthrope* at the Young Vic in a modern adaptation and she was very funny and stylish. I thought Elizabeth's persona and accent were right for someone who is different from the other characters. After all, Marguerite is very much the odd one out in England.

'We wanted to play up the fact that Chauvelin is older than Robespierre. We wanted that past history of Chauvelin and Marguerite so we were looking for a slightly older man with a younger woman. Whilst Chauvelin is a villainous part, he also has a heart, as you see in the previous love affair and sexual frisson with Marguerite. Martin Shaw fitted every requirement.'

Julian Murphy adds: 'Martin was the last of three to be cast. We didn't want an obvious villain because Chauvelin is more than a villain. He's a character you sometimes have sympathy for and whilst he can be monstrous, you also see another side that was once in love with Marguerite – and still is, if the truth be told. It was very important not to do the obvious when casting Chauvelin. People don't automatically see Martin as a villain – which is to our advantage. He's also brilliant at action which is handy because Chauvelin does a lot of fighting.

'Patrick bears all the credit for casting Elizabeth. I had always thought of her as an American film actress until he mentioned her performance in *The Misanthrope*. When she came in, we immediately knew she was right, although she was worried because she was pregnant and wasn't sure how it would fit in with filming. In the end, it worked out well for everyone.

Martin Shaw fulfilled all the requirements for Chauvelin.

'Our only reservation with Richard was whether he would want to do it. He's got such a successful film career that we weren't sure whether we would be able to persuade him to do television on a scale which he hasn't done for a long time. But he obviously liked the part and I think he also enjoyed the speed of the filming process. There's no doubt that he's a real coup. He's so natural. Many actors would have asked, "Why does this guy do these things?" But Richard's managed to make the character seem so instinctive, natural and right. And his performance on screen bears that out.'

Everyone on the production waxes lyrical about filming in the Czech Republic – a director's dream with hardly any telegraph poles and no satellite dishes. 'We had an embarrassment of riches in the Czech Republic,' says Julian Murphy, 'three or four choices for most locations. There were extraordinary locations which we could usually have only dreamed about. For instance, in a country of around 10 million people, there are something like 2,500 castles,

Krivoklat Castle in the Czech Republic dressed up to stage the battle of Cholet.

which was ideal for our purposes. So much of the country is period. Most roads in the old parts are cobbled with no road markings and the majority of the street lights are at least as old as the early nineteenth century. We had to take bits out and put in candles to make them period but it was far easier than covering up a lamp-post. Even the lightning conductors are period in some places! There is a shot in the first film which takes in the rooftops of old Prague (it is supposed to be a shot of the whole of Paris) and we didn't have to touch a thing.

'There were very few locations that were difficult to find. The Palais de Justice was a bit tricky but we eventually settled on Salmovsky Palace, by Prague Castle. And the main Paris street that Patrick wanted for the guillotine and rescue which is the climax to episode one, he eventually found in Zatec – a town in the north-west of the country. We were able to close six or seven streets there and they were virtually all period with hardly any changes needed. An old German Jewish synagogue, which must have had an interesting history, became the main hall of La Force prison and we managed to find a superb little Baroque theatre at a place called Litomysl. It was virtually untouched and was still candlelit with the original backdrops and original stage machinery – things you don't find anywhere.

'In fact, the biggest problem was pronouncing the locations. There were at least three or four locations which the unit never managed to pronounce and which became known as things like "JR". They're very short of vowels, the Czechs, so we spent much

An old German Jewish synagogue at Zatec was converted into La Force prison.

of our time at locations we couldn't name!'

For Patrick Lau, filming in the Czech Republic simply got better and better. 'When I first went out there on a recce to see whether the Cezch Republic was the right location for us, it was in the depth of winter and we toured the whole country in about three days to find key places for battles and castles – places that could double as Paris and as the countryside for the Vendée rebellion. But as soon as I saw the possibilities of the castles and the bits of Prague which could be turned into eighteenth-century Paris, I knew this was the place. The films have a huge sense of scale and colour which we wouldn't have been able to do in Britain or France. After ten weeks' filming in the Czech Republic, I came back to London to film at our Blakeney Hall in Hertfordshire and heard aeroplane noise and motorway noise which stopped me filming. I had almost forgotten what it sounded like because there was none of that in the Czech Republic.

'The schedule of thirty days for each film was only possible due to the ease of filming out there. For instance, we were filming outside in Salmovsky Palace square – the equivalent of Buckingham Palace in London – for three nights and two days. That would have been impossible in London. For Cholet, where we staged our big Vendée battle in episode two, we filmed at Krivoklat Castle, an hour from Prague. I knew that I could shoot 360 degrees with 150 extras and nothing out of period. It was glorious. We had to negotiate, of course, but most of the castle owners need the money from filming to carry out renovations so their prices are generally practical and reasonable for a TV budget. Whereas in France and Britain, even if you found such a place, there would be so many restrictions, often because people still live there. I can honestly say I've never felt so fulfilled by a period piece.'

To underline Patrick's point, the most difficult location to find in the entire production was a period English ballroom and when somewhere suitable was unearthed, permission to film was refused. As the search proved ever more fruitless, it was finally decided to build a ballroom at the unit's Czech base, the famous Barrandov studios in Prague, Hitler's old propaganda studios and the place where influential Czech-born director Milos Forman made some of his best-known films in the 1960s.

The battle of Cholet took five days to film, complete with horses, guns, musket fire, hand-to-hand fighting and extras scaling the 100ft-high castle walls. But for unintentional drama and confusion, it was overshadowed by the mass riot in Paris, filmed at night in Salmovsky Palace square. 'It was a spectacular scene,' recalls Patrick Lau, 'with Percy carrying out a typically daring rescue through the mayhem of the crowds with muskets firing and carts burning. The main problem was the muskets. It's surprising anyone was ever killed in the past! They

The picturesque entrance to Krivoklat Castle.

The battle of Cholet took five days to film.

Chauvelin's musket fire lights up the night sky as he attempts to foil the Pimpernel.

never seem to fire, and reloading and resetting them takes a long time while you wait for the flint to spark off the gunpowder. And when they do go off, they go off like a cannon.

'For this riot scene, we had 100 Czech extras and because we only loaded the gunpowder for the actual takes, during the camera rehearsal we said to the extras, "If it is your turn to fire, say 'bang'" so that I would know out of 100 people exactly where the camera should be pointing. But on one take, when an extra's musket didn't fire properly, he still shouted at the camera, "Bang!" It was rather sweet to show he remembered his cue... '

The Czech extras became bywords for enthusiasm. In some locations, whole towns would turn out to watch filming, usually in the hope of being able to take part. In Litomysl, when a call was put out to the locals, 300 hopefuls turned up when only 200 extras were needed. Costume designer Howard Burden had little choice but to put the names in a hat and draw lots.

'The Czech crowds were always extremely well behaved,' adds Patrick Lau, 'but language could be a bit of a problem. And with action scenes involving horses, any lack of understanding can be dangerous so you have to rely on the translator. Since Czechs speak little English, it became quite time-consuming.'

For economic reasons and to cut down on travelling time, the production unit chose three principal bases in the Czech Republic – Prague, Zatec and Brno, the latter being to the south-east of Prague and near the battle site of Austerlitz where Napoleon led the French to a famous victory over the combined might of Russia and Austria in 1805. Although much of the country lends itself to period filming, there was still plenty of work to be done by production designer Tim Hutchinson and his team before the Czech Republic was ready to play eighteenth-century France.

'I had to learn about the French Revolution very quickly,' he says, 'because my previous knowledge of that period was fairly limited. But by studying prints from books, I was able to build up an accurate picture of what the Paris of the Pimpernel must have looked like. Architecturally, some of the buildings in the Czech Republic lean towards the Baroque period which was slightly earlier so, technically speaking, they weren't quite right, but because *The Scarlet Pimpernel* is a fantasy piece, I allowed myself some leeway. The existing colours and texture of the buildings work well so it was a case of covering up the modern bits – things like air conditioning, road signs and modern windows. All the glass in those days was quite small – the largest pane size was 15 inches by 12 inches – so anything bigger on screen would have been a giveaway.

'In addition, I wanted to capture the feel of Revolutionary Paris so I introduced bunting in the streets, as well as a sense of unease and unrest. So there would be mobs everywhere, lots of smoke and plenty of background shots of people skulking in doorways, hiding in fear of their lives. Although the popular myth about the

Muskets which were reluctant to fire proved a constant headache for the production team, especially in crowd scenes.

Right: Production designer Tim Hutchinson and (below) his design drawing for the Carlton House ball. Far right: Edward Bennett directs Czech extras in episode three.

Revolution is that only the aristocracy went to the guillotine, the ordinary people also lived in fear. There is a true account of seven people needing to be guillotined one day but because the authorities could only find five, they dragged the other two out of the crowd. So nobody knew when it would be their turn. In order to present a nice contrast with smoky, grimy Paris, I've deliberately portrayed England as clean and sterile.

'For Krivoklat, which doubles as Cholet, I wanted to give the castle a French feel.

Playing a game of Battledore at the ball.

The face of the castle was very white with Bohemian decoration so I set about making it look more evil. To do that, we built large wooden buttresses along which the soldiers could patrol and which also proved a useful vantage point for lighting. Basically, I made the place look a bit more sinister, to fit in with the story. We also had to carry out adjustments to the theatre at Litomysl which was over 200 years old. We were extremely lucky to find – and to be able to use – somewhere like that and it didn't need too much in the way of dressing. But we painted new backdrops, repositioned the front curtains for our filming requirements and added period stage lights. We also built a set of the backstage area.

'The principal set we had to build, however, was the 75ft by 40ft English ballroom modelled on Carlton House, which used to be by The Mall in London. All that's left of it now are the columns which support the National Gallery. That set was built at the Barrandov studios, so it was interesting for the Czech construction crew to build a lavish English ballroom, and they did a terrific job. We also built the interior of Sir Percy's yacht, the *Daydream*, in Prague, although the exteriors were done in Cornwall. We found an old French fishing boat dating from around the turn of the century, and with really nice lines. We made special windows for it, smartened it up and added painted cut-outs to represent ornate carvings. It looked quite smart

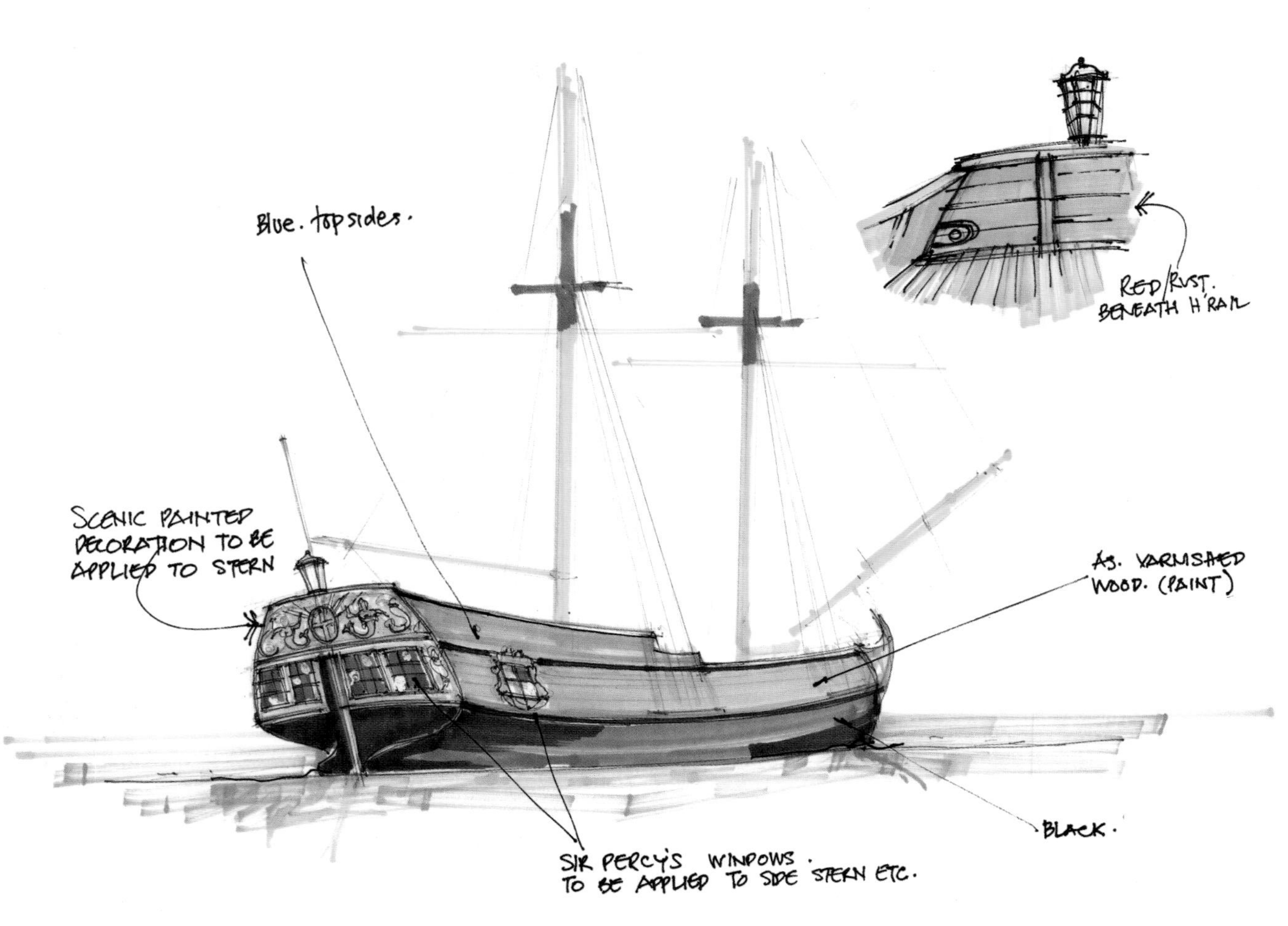

The design drawings for Sir Percy's yacht, the Daydream.

when it was finished.'

Other Czech locations included Slavkov castle, the site of the battle of Austerlitz, which served as Robespierre's office, and a rocky area some one and a half hours from Prague which played the Vendée woods. The crew even filmed in the Prague sewers for the Pimpernel's raid on the Palais de Justice. 'We used the genuine brick-vaulted city sewers,' says Tim Hutchinson, 'which are still in use today. Fortunately they carried rainwater not sewage, but if it had started to rain we would have had to get out pretty quickly. Luckily, it didn't.'

Opposite top: Props assembled for scenes at Carlton House. Below: Actor Jonathan Coy poses for his portrait as the Prince of Wales and (left) the finished article.

One of the biggest obstacles to be overcome was the sheer logistical exercise of transporting props, costumes and even horses to Prague. For whilst some items were obtainable locally, the majority had to be shipped over from England. Five horses were taken out for the principal cast members but the rest were Czech, and five composite carriages were brought along, which, with a little adaptation, could be converted into twice that number for big crowd scenes. But the crew struck lucky with the tumbrils, the carts which were used to transport victims to the guillotine. 'We had one big cart,'

reveals Tim Hutchinson, 'but otherwise we simply adapted existing Czech farm carts. It was a stroke of fortune that they are so similar to the eighteenth-century tumbrils.'

The French period furniture was imported from London specialist suppliers, as were most of the high society props, with the exception of the chandeliers and glass, which were superb Czech crystal.

'We had to make some props ourselves,' adds Tim Hutchinson. 'We made period proclamations which were handwritten on distressed paper and we made a game of battledore, which was like badminton but played with two paddles and two large shuttles. There is also a scene where a statue of Louis XV is pulled down so we built two statues of Louis – one in lightweight polystyrene, the other in plaster. On the plaster model, the head was loose. We began by putting the polystyrene statue on a pedestal and having it pulled off by ropes. As it toppled, we replaced it with the plaster one and cut to that. The idea was that Louis's head would come off and fortunately it worked first time although we had quantities of glue on standby to stick it back on if we had needed to do a second take.

'We also had to commission artists to paint portraits of the Prince of Wales and Robespierre to be hung on walls. But of course we didn't want paintings of the real Prince or Robespierre – we wanted portraits of the actors playing them. So we needed Jonathan Coy in costume as the Prince and Ronan Vibert as Robespierre. In these cases, you always hope that the actor is cast in time.'

But inevitably the most talked-about props on *The Scarlet Pimpernel* were the guillotines. 'We had two guillotines,' says producer Julian Murphy, 'a portable one (modelled on the guillotine which is in a museum at Lyons) and a static one. Both were made at Barrandov. The static one stands on a rostrum in the square and the mobile

A variety of carriages and carts, some adapted from Czech farm carts, have been used on the production.

Opposite: Sparkling chandeliers illuminate the set of the grand ball.

The cutting edges of the specially-made guillotines were tested on marrows rather than actors.

one, which we painted black to make it look suitably sinister, is drawn by two horses – black, of course. They're slightly larger than they were in reality. It's interesting that our image of a guillotine standing 20ft high in a square is entirely due to film-makers. In fact, they were only about 7ft high, but they were mounted on high platforms. Since our films are meant for family entertainment, there are no explicit scenes of heads being parted from bodies but the blades are metal and sharp enough to exercise caution. And they work, but we chose to test them on marrows rather than actors!'

The task of creating and acquiring the mountain of costumes for *The Scarlet Pimpernel* fell to costume designer Howard Burden, who worked with director Patrick Lau on *Invasion: Earth* and the pilot of *McCallum*. 'It has been a monumental exercise,' says Howard. 'In the first two episodes alone, there were something like 3,500 extras and so we took out to Prague 800 costumes which were worn again and again. We've had articulated truck loads of costumes and we've also had to send stuff by air. We've had a warehouse full of costumes, hats, shoes and accessories because if you've got 200 extras in on one day, you need that amount in stock. So it's really been like having a travelling costume hire company.

'We've had the principals' costumes made specially, both in England and the Czech Republic, but we had to get the vast majority of extras' costumes from three London costume companies because, unlike Britain, the Czech Republic has no tradition of costume film-making so there are few costumes to draw on. And for all the scenes with stunt doubles, we needed two of each costume. What made the whole operation even more complicated was that there were two other period productions, *Hornblower* and *Vanity Fair*, being made at the same time so a lot of the stuff was out and you find yourself scrambling around for boots etcetera.

'Before I could start, I had to research the French Revolution, which was a particularly interesting period costume-wise because it was so transitory. In a short time, the whole style of costume changed. The powdered wigs and elaborate costumes became more simplified, but not like the Empire Line of the Napoleonic era. So I did a lot of research. I went to the Louvre in Paris and studied oil paintings and books of paintings from that period and I also visited the Victoria and Albert Museum in

London. From there, it was a question of taking that style and putting it on a modern body because the shape is different now. Height is the major difference – people are much taller now than they were in the 1790s.

'It was a tremendously romantic period for costumes and much more flamboyant for men than for women. The French peasant men usually wore a shirt, breeches, a waistcoat, a cutaway coat with rough boots or old shoes and stockings. Most had a necktie and all wore a hat. In the course of the three films, we used over 300 hats, some of which were hired and the rest made. The aristocrats also wore shirt, breeches, waistcoat and cutaway coat but with smart buckled shoes. And the coat would have a high collar – very peacock in style. The women's clothes were slightly less decorative – it was a real dandy period. Lower-class women basically wore anything they could get their hands on so we've reflected that by dressing our extras in skirts with a bodice and some sort of chemise but topped with a man's coat or waistcoat – quite anarchic. The upper classes wore very fitted clothes with a tight bodice, full skirts and corsets which showed off an ample bosom. They looked very pretty.

'After I had completed my research, I drew up costume designs for each of the major characters. Then I presented the look of the character's costume to the director so that he could visualise it and then I showed the artists. It's important to liaise closely

The orchestra illustrate the costumes and wigs of the period.

with the artists because it's when they're in costume that they develop their character. The women's costumes for that period were quite corsetted so it's an effort to wear that all day, but you need the corsetting to get the right shape because it makes the actresses hold themselves in a different way.

'When the design was finished, it was a matter of sampling for authentic-looking fabrics and trim and lace. We had an army of costume-makers to make them at the Barrandov workshop but we had to ship out the fabrics because you can't get them out

Costume designer Howard Burden's drawings for one of Marguerite's dresses and one of Sir Percy's costumes.

there. However, the tailoring skills there are excellent.

'With Richard E. Grant, Elizabeth McGovern, Martin Shaw and the other main members of cast, we had everything made from scratch, right down to things like riding hats and boots. The trick when you have clothes made as new is not to make them look new on screen. After all, nobody goes around wearing brand new clothes all the time. So it is one of the ironies of my job that, after having these costumes made, I set about wrecking them! To make them look worn-in, we employed a variety of methods. We broke the clothes down with powders and sprays and we also rubbed the collars with a cheese-grater to create a shredded effect. And we dipped all the whites in tea for a yellowed, ageing look!

With as many as 200 extras involved in a single day's filming, acquiring and transporting costumes was a huge logistic exercise.

'We didn't use anything which was genuinely authentic from the period because nobody would be wild enough to lend it. There's old lace and old trimmings and old buttons but anything else would be too fragile.'

One of Howard's most intriguing assignments was creating the right look for actress and opera singer La Touraine, who dresses as a man to become the feared Chevalier d'Orly. 'When she's fighting, nobody is supposed to know that she's a woman so we disguised actress Suzanne Bertish in the same breeches, waistcoat, high stock and cutaway coat that the male characters wore. And then, for her female counterpart, we emphasised her prettiness as a contrast.

'The Czech extras were also a challenge. I have to say that they were extremely understanding, patient and impeccably behaved, but some of the walk-ons we used in Prague were recruited from the local down-and-outs. A lot of them were homeless. As a result, you'd fit them with their costume one day but then the next day when you were ready to film them, you'd find that they'd simply wandered off to another part of town because they had no roots. They were nowhere to be found. So we'd have a few costumes with nobody to fill them. This meant hastily recruiting more extras of approximately the same build to the ones that had gone missing. It certainly kept us on our toes.'

Make-up designer Pam Haddock confesses that she has been a model of restraint on *The Scarlet Pimpernel*. 'In the past, I've worked on shows like *Casualty* and *McCallum* where there is plenty of blood and guts and, given the number of people who were executed, butchered and tortured during the French Revolution, I was looking forward to preparing some nice juicy wounds. But I had to hold myself back and remember that it's supposed to be aimed at a family audience.

Elizabeth McGovern receives final touches from make-up.

'Even the scene in episode one where Minette is discovered with her throat cut is artistic. I had a nasty-looking prosthetic piece ready to stick on to actress Emilia Fox but I couldn't use it. I had to settle for a bit of blood trickling down her arm. It was a shame! And when Father Joseph was tortured in episode two, I wanted to give him swollen eyes, plenty of blood, the full works. But in the end, I had to settle for a few wounds and bruises and some proprietary blood matted in his hair, although I did make sure that actor Robert Langdon Lloyd didn't shave for a day or two so that he had a growth of stubble, which you would expect from someone who had been held captive. That helped make him look rougher.

'I had worked with Patrick Lau, who directed the first two episodes, on *McCallum* and he knew I could be quirky about my approach. And he encouraged me to be bold, to do my own thing within reason. For he was adamant that he didn't want *The Scarlet Pimpernel* to look like any other BBC drama. So I took risks, like giving Millie Fox a cropped hairstyle. I am sure I'll get letters from viewers complaining that the style is too modern, but some Republican women did wear their hair that short. It was a weird period where, for the sansculottes, anything went.

'I was also able to be outrageous with Mazzarini's party. From the script, I could see it was meant to be a pretty wild party so I picked out some wonderfully weird wigs – blue ones, pink ones and big white plaited ones. Having studied the art of the time, I knew how far I could go.

'Wigs have been a major part of my job on *The Scarlet Pimpernel* and once I'd sorted out the individual looks with Patrick Lau, I took the principal actors in to Wig Specialities in London. Wig Specialities have been brilliant – they've pulled out all the stops for me because on one day alone, I took out 200 wigs. Apart from Jamie Bamber who is young and for whom we were able to create a newer look with his own hair, all of the cast have worn either wigs or backpieces. Richard E. Grant and Martin Shaw both had backpieces – extra sections of hair added to their own at the back. As they are like extensions, you have to match the colour precisely to the actor's own hair and, of course, you have to get the shape right too. If the actor has wavy hair, there's no use

Beth Goddard as Suzanne de Tournay, resplendent in fine wig.

A blazing cart spares Marguerite from the guillotine in episode one.

adding on a straight backpiece because it will stick out like a sore thumb. Elizabeth McGovern was keen to wear a wig so we pinned up her hair beneath it. In fact, she had three – two for everyday use and one for parties. For Suzanne Bertish, who played La Touraine and the Chevalier, I had to create two distinctive looks. When she was playing the man, I used her own hair with a small piece added and filled in her eyebrows. And she didn't wear any make-up. But for the woman, I put her in a white wig and accentuated her femininity with false eyelashes.

'By way of a contrast to the styles of the Revolution, the very first scene is a tea which is set in pre-Revolution 1780. So for that I was able to incorporate a different look – big powdered wigs with white painted faces and patches stuck on the faces. That was fun. The biggest scene for me was the Carlton House ball. We brought five hair and make-up artists out to Prague from England, making a total of ten of us in all. Since it was set in England, I wanted the characters in that scene to look light and vibrant as a contrast to the French who I've made look very fluffy and dark. I've kept the French characters dark. When they were looking for Czech extras to play the sansculottes, I asked for as many people with beards as possible because it made for a slightly more sinister look.'

Pam's recurring nightmare was that wigs might go missing in transit. 'With having to transport hundreds of wigs and backpieces from London to Prague, my dread was that some would go missing on the journey. If something like Richard E. Grant's backpiece got lost, we'd have been in a right mess, but fortunately everything always arrived safe and sound. It was a huge relief.'

One of the first tasks for many of the cast of *The Scarlet Pimpernel* was to brush up on their horse-riding skills. The principals' horses were supplied by stunt co-ordinator Steve Dent, whose family have been in the film business since 1945 and who has a stock of seventy horses at his farm at Rickmansworth in Hertfordshire. He says: 'Whenever we start a project, we always insist that the actors come to us for riding tuition so that we can select a suitable horse for them. And after a few lessons, all of the cast of *The Scarlet Pimpernel* were up to riding their horses. When we buy horses to supply film companies, we go for good looks and, more importantly, good manners.'

Steve, who also supplied the carriages from the stock of over 300 horse-drawn vehicles kept at his home, was responsible for all of the stunts on the three films. Among the most spectacular was the burning cart diversion which enabled the Pimpernel to perform one of his dramatic rescues. The cart was fitted with propane gas taps which could be switched on and off when needed but which gave the illusion of a real fire. This created a controlled and relatively safe environment for cast and crew without damaging the actual cart should it be required for another take. As an added precaution, the cart was surrounded by stunt men wearing flameproof clothing under their costumes. 'That's the key to stunts,' says Steve, 'making them look dangerous on screen but ensuring that they are safe to do.'

Working with Steve Dent was sword master Terry Walsh, who used to be Michael Caine's screen double and who has worked on such productions as *The Saint*, *The Avengers*, *The Persuaders*, *Doctor Who*, *Robin of Sherwood*, *Henry V* (with Kenneth Branagh) and *Robin Hood – Prince of Thieves*. 'My job is to make sure the artists are safe, to train the stunt doubles and to make sure the fights look good. People think screen fights are just thrown together but I carefully choreograph them and insist that they are in character. My instructions regarding the Pimpernel were simply: clinical. Because that's what he is – a clinical, ruthless fighter. He's also an expert swordsman and, as a member of the aristocracy, he tends to fight clean. Chauvelin, on the other hand, is quite prepared to fight dirty. So when Percy and Chauvelin have an encounter, it begins with a sword fight but ends with a kick fight, Chauvelin reverting to type by kicking Percy in the shins. That's what I mean about the fights being in character – I try to get a fight to be like dialogue.

Director Patrick Lau makes a point to sword master Terry Walsh.

Above: Sword master Terry Walsh (right) supervises a fight scene involving Henri (James Callis).

Right: Production crew and Czech extras look on as director Patrick Lau (second from right) prepares a fight scene.

Richard E. Grant proved a quick learner with a sword.

'We had fights with all manner of weapons on *The Scarlet Pimpernel* – rifles, bayonets, swords, pitchforks, clubs, tree branches and hand-to-hand. We got the rifles and bayonets from Prague but the swords were brought over from England. We didn't use retractable swords but we did have retractable knives and some muskets were real while others were dummies. Since most of the peasants wouldn't have had weapons, we armed them with agricultural implements like rubber pitchforks made up by the art department.

'The main cast all had doubles. Richard E. Grant did some fight scenes. I think he was a bit worried about doing them but he was actually very good – a quick learner. He had a particularly good posture and was able to act and fight at the same time, which isn't easy. Martin Shaw had done a little fencing in the past and was very keen to do sword fights. He does kick boxing so, like Richard, he's got a very good posture. The only trouble was, his previous experience had been with a different type of sword so he had to readjust because his fingers were the wrong way round. I tended to give the brute force stuff to Anthony Green, who plays Sir Andrew, because he's a big lad.'

The Pimpernel's fighting prowess is always to the fore. Terry says: 'For the scene where he escapes from his prison cell, he has to kill three French soldiers in just fifteen seconds. It was a question of getting the timing right within the confines of the set and without making it look contrived and silly. So he starts off by breaking one guy's neck and takes it from there. It all worked out well and it was in character. That's the joy of arranging fights for a fighting machine like the Scarlet Pimpernel.'

CHAPTER SIX

THE ETERNAL TRIANGLE

Sir Percy Blakeney

Soon after his birth in 1760, his mother Joan became mentally unstable and his father, Algenon, took her to France to recuperate, leaving the infant Percy in the care of his grandfather. When Percy was five, his grandfather died and the boy rejoined his parents in Paris. The reunion was a disaster since Joan's health had not improved and Algenon was plagued with depression, so Percy returned to England, this time in the care of his widowed cousin, Anne.

The high-spirited boy ran wild and retreated into his imagination. Lacking the concentration for book learning, he developed a talent for sport and, through his visits to his parents, spoke impeccable French. In the course of these visits, he made friends with the son of some family friends, Philippe de Saint-Cyr. With Philippe, Percy took fencing lessons and became a brilliant swordsman.

Percy's mother died when he was ten. He returned to England with his father but Algenon was unable to cope with the boy and sent him to Harrow before returning to Paris. At Harrow, Percy developed friendships with Andrew Ffoulkes, Anthony Dewhurst and William Pitt which were to last a lifetime. The last-named encouraged Percy academically and soon his record improved.

Algenon Blakeney died in 1775 and, at fifteen, Percy became a baronet in charge of a vast fortune. Disregarding the advice of his schoolmasters, Percy exploited his title and turned into a moneyed gentleman about town. He earned a reputation for being a fashionable and amusing sophisticate and became a great favourite of the Prince Regent. Meanwhile William Pitt had entered politics and Percy, through his connections, was instrumental in securing Pitt's elevation to Chancellor of the Exchequer. Pitt urged Percy to enter Parliament but Percy was disillusioned with politics, frustrated that his attempts to address the problems of poverty and unemployment met with indifference.

Sickened by seeing so many of his friends go to the guillotine, Sir Percy Blakeney embarked on a mission of mercy.

In 1787 Percy became engaged to the Hon. Mary de Courcy but was devastated to learn that Mary was a gold-digger, eager to ensnare the richest, most eligible man in England. Breaking off the engagement, he revisited Paris where he made himself useful to Pitt (now Prime Minister) by reporting back to him on the latest political happenings. By posing as an urbane Englishman, Percy was able to mix with the new revolutionaries and acquire valuable intelligence information. In March 1789 he attended a gala performance at the Théâtre des Arts where he met the celebrated actress, Marguerite Saint-Just. He continued to spy for Pitt but found himself falling helplessly in love with Marguerite. Believing that Marguerite would never consent to marry him, Percy left Paris and travelled to India but eventually returned, determined to make her his wife. To his delight, she accepted his proposal of marriage and the couple were wed in March 1792.

Owing to Marguerite's theatre commitments, they honeymooned in Paris where Percy's happiness was wrecked when he heard that his wife was implicated in the execution of his friends, the Saint-Cyrs. At the same time, he was sickened by the petty corruptions and outrageous trials that were becoming commonplace in France. Not prepared to see another of his friends go to the guillotine, Percy carried out a daring rescue and secured his friend's passage to England and safety.

Reinstated at Blakeney Hall in Richmond, Percy's suspicions of Marguerite continued to grow. Believing that she had married him for an entrée into English society and its political advantages, he finally confronted her about her part in the death of the Saint-Cyrs, only to be shocked by her proud confirmation and lack of remorse. Although still in love with her, Percy began to avoid her company while maintaining the public pretence of marriage.

With Andrew Ffoulkes, Percy devised a plan to confound the revolutionary tribunals by rescuing more innocent people from the guillotine. The Scarlet Pimpernel was born and the League founded. Sir Percy was determined to conceal his dual identity from Marguerite and accounted for his frequent absences by inventing hunting trips and the like. Also unbeknown to Marguerite, her brother Armand became the League of the Scarlet Pimpernel's man in Paris.

Lady Marguerite Blakeney

Born in 1769, Marguerite Saint-Just was brought up in the provinces where her father, Valentin, worked on the estate of the Marquis de Saint-Cyr. Valentin Saint-Just was a charismatic character and a radical thinker and inspired loyalty among a small group of locals campaigning for social justice. The Marquis de Saint-Cyr resorted to extreme measures to crush the insurrection and had Valentin and his wife Colette

The enigmatic Lady Marguerite – darling of fashionable society.

publicly executed. The fifteen-year-old Marguerite and her brother Armand, twenty-three, were forced to watch this horror. That night, after a drunken celebration, the Marquis's son Philippe, accompanied by a group of young aristocrats, broke into the Saint-Just cottage, raped Marguerite and flogged Armand. This dreadful deed confirmed her political convictions.

Marguerite and her brother fled to Lyons where Armand took what work he could get and Marguerite found herself drawn to the theatre, where her beauty and natural talents flourished, bringing her growing acclaim. To further Marguerite's ambitions, they moved to Paris in 1788, seeking out their cousin, Louis Saint-Just, a prominent figure in the worlds of politics and art. Through his influence, Marguerite obtained a minor role at the Théâtre des Arts but quickly went on to become a leading lady and the darling of fashionable society. She attracted a coterie that was as brilliant as it was exclusive, but entrance into her salon was determined by talent and intellect rather than by money or title. Known to be an ardent Republican, she became host to many political debates during the period of revolutionary fervour.

Although charming and hospitable, Marguerite's experience at the hands of Philippe Saint-Cyr had made her mistrustful and she maintained an elusive quality. She was besieged with proposals of marriage but no suitor was granted more than friendship until she met the intriguing Englishman, Sir Percy Blakeney. He spoke little, never joining in the political discussions, but any suspicions she may have harboured were allayed by his perfect manners, elegant diction and extensive knowledge of her country and countrymen. Also, she was sure that behind his outward flippancy lay a brilliant mind and strong character. For the best part of a year, Sir Percy was her constant companion until, without a word, he left Paris.

For over twelve months, Marguerite heard nothing from Sir Percy. During this time, her friendship with one of her erstwhile suitors, Paul Chauvelin, a politician with a shrewd and cunning mind, grew. Revolutionary zeal prompted a bitter mistrust of the French upper classes and during one of her soirées, she heard of the Marquis de Saint-Cyr's involvement in an appeal to the Austrian Emperor for his help in quashing the Republican movement. Motivated by a combination of revenge and ideology, Marguerite informed Chauvelin of Saint-Cyr's treacherous overtures. Within 24 hours, Saint-Cyr had been arrested and damning evidence found in his possession. There was a showcase trial after which Saint-Cyr, his wife and two sons (but not the daughter Angèle, who escaped to England) were beheaded while Marguerite watched.

Shortly afterwards, Sir Percy returned to Paris and enchanted Marguerite with tales of his travels to the East. When he professed his utter devotion to her, she agreed to marry him but she soon had misgivings about the union. Returning home late from the theatre, she would find her husband either absent or asleep. The passionate nature she had hoped to discover dissolved into indifference, exacerbated by her feeling unable to tell him the reasons behind her betrayal of the Saint-Cyr family. As the emotional distance between them grew, Marguerite felt increasingly isolated in London. Armand's visits were eagerly anticipated and when, in September 1792, Chauvelin arrived in London as the French Ambassador, she was happy to renew his acquaintance.

Chauvelin

Born around 1750, Paul Chauvelin never knew who his real parents were. Adopted as a baby, he was brought up by the otherwise childless Comte and Comtesse de Bonnefin and, although he never wanted for anything, he was a lonely child, always feeling slightly out of place. He was encouraged to study for the priesthood but soon discovered that this was not his calling, preferring instead to keep the company of the ladies and brigands at a nearby brothel. When these nocturnal activities were revealed,

Chauvelin was thrown out of the monastery and disowned by his adopted parents.

With nothing to his name but the clothes he was wearing, Chauvelin made his way to Paris. His cunning and intelligence secured him a position as a legal clerk where he ingratiated himself with both clients and colleagues. As his circle of influence grew, he gained an entry into society and an insight into the world of politics. Since he perceived that future power would lie in the hands of the Republicans, he allied himself to their cause, becoming a prominent member of the Jacobin clubs.

Although he enjoyed the company of women, Chauvelin never married, considering a wife to be an unnecessary distraction from his ambitions. There was only one woman for whom he would have made an exception – Marguerite Saint-Just – but when the actress married an English aristocrat, Chauvelin was as surprised as the rest of Parisian society and secretly nursed a bitter disappointment. However, Chauvelin's political shrewdness was rewarded and in 1792 he was appointed Ambassador to England with the specific goal of revealing the identity of the man known as the Scarlet Pimpernel.

Lord Tony (Jamie Bamber) is captured by Fumier and Chauvelin.

CHAPTER SEVEN

WHISPERS FROM ABROAD

Richard E. Grant as Sir Percy Blakeney

Ask Richard E. Grant what appealed to him about playing the Scarlet Pimpernel and his reply is typically honest. 'I get to play somebody who kisses people, seduces people, is married, kills bad people and saves good people! So instead of classical story types of being the bad guy who doesn't get the girl and who possibly gets killed in the end, this is real *Boys' Own* stuff.'

Richard was the ideal choice to play the Pimpernel. He is very good at the foppish comedy; he can do the action. And even while he talks twenty to the dozen, you can see almost see his brain working overtime, always one step ahead. He may be physically sitting in his film-set trailer, but his mind is constantly racing off elsewhere in the same way that while Sir Percy is entertaining society guests in London, he is secretly planning his next rescue mission in Paris.

'I love the double life that the Pimpernel enjoys,' he continues, 'and the idea of the audience knowing who he is and what he's up to but of other people not knowing. That's a great source of humour and tension. The Pimpernel is like an eighteenth-century Bruce Wayne or Clark Kent. On the one side, there's this ridiculous person and on the other, a wholly plausible man who saves people. The amount of screen time which we devote to the fop side is less than in previous versions – it's not half and half so the idea that this man is a very privileged person going to save other privileged people is lessened in some way. And I'm sure that's a nod to television today with people's shortening attention spans (they want more action scenes) as well as a political thing about this overpowdered mannequin going over to save mankind in France.

'The Pimpernel is driven by a sense of justice but also because he's a kind of adrenaline junkie who gets off on the fact that he's led a very privileged life and suffered the boredom that can go with that, but who can also pit himself against Robespierre and the whole French Revolution. It's so preposterous. But he has this

The Pimpernel's double identity held tremendous appeal for Richard E. Grant.

suicidal, devil-may-care side to his personality and I think the character's enduring appeal is partly down to the fact that he leads a double life because that is something which everyone can identify with to some degree. It may also go some way to explaining why there is this apparent global obsession with actors and their private lives. It seems to me that it's the part that actors play that is interesting about them whereas their private lives tend not to be anything like as interesting. But there is this constant fascination – you want to know. You see somebody as one thing and you think there must be something else that you just don't know about. It's this thing about everybody having a private face. As soon as the Scarlet Pimpernel is a man of action, there is no room for his fancy-pants routine. It's straight into "get out of the way or I'll kill you".

'He's a man who doesn't really take himself that seriously although what he does is very serious. There's an Oscar Wilde quote about being terribly serious about frivolity and frivolous about serious things and that to me sums up the Scarlet Pimpernel's sensibility. And there is a lot of humour in the stories which makes them tangible for an audience today.'

Richard admits that his prior knowledge of the character was sparse. 'All I knew about the Pimpernel was the poem: "They seek him here, they seek him there..." I'd never read the books and whilst I had seen the Leslie Howard film when I was a child, I hadn't seen any other versions. When I knew I was going to be playing the Pimpernel, I tried to get hold of the David Niven version but it wasn't available. However, from the Leslie Howard film I had been able to see a 1930s sensibility of what the English and French aristocracy were. The narrative drive of the character isn't affected by when the film is made, which I suppose is another part of the Pimpernel's timeless appeal, although the idea of a guy in a frock-coat saving aristocrats, or indeed anybody, in the inter-war years has a very different notion to nowadays.

'I didn't do any great historical research because there is no record of the Pimpernel ever existing – he's a fantasy character, made up by the Baroness. He's the product of a Hungarian writer creating her ideal English gentleman so it's already in the realms of fantasy. Doing it as a film is much grander than the reality of the French Revolution. Then there was a guillotine which chopped people's heads off – it didn't produce bunches of flowers at the other end!'

Richard E. Grant (the E stands for Esterhuysen) was born in 1957 in Mbabane, the capital of Swaziland, where his father was Minister for Education. It was a capital of just three streets and Richard remembers the installation of the first traffic light on the main street in 1964 and how the whole town came to stare at it. As a child, he made his own cardboard theatre and, at the age of eight, wrote a play. He subsequently progressed to having a proper marionette theatre in the garage. It was pretty obvious that he wanted to act. After his parents split up when Richard was eleven, he joined an amateur dramatic society as a teenager and started his own multi-racial theatre troupe before finally coming to England to try his luck in 1982.

A few months after arriving in England, he met dialect coach Joan Washington to whom he has now been happily married for eleven years. They have a nine-year-old daughter, Olivia. 'The film industry is full of unhappy people,' he remarks. 'It just makes me realise how lucky I am to have someone I am still besotted with sixteen years after we met. And however much you love your job, it never loves you back in the same way. There always has to be something over and above the love of your profession – and for me that is my wife and daughter.'

The Pimpernel can be serious or frivolous as the fancy takes him.

Success didn't come immediately in England. In 1986 he was another struggling actor until writer/director Bruce Robinson cast him opposite Paul McGann in *Withnail and I*, a film which has gone on to become a cult classic. 'I was rising thirty and had been chronically, esteem-decimatingly unemployed for nine months. I was sent for an audition with Bruce Robinson. Daniel Day-Lewis, to whom I'm eternally grateful, had turned down Withnail. Ken Branagh was after it but I gather I got the part because of the way I read one line.'

Soon Richard began to corner the market in eccentric, oddball film roles such as a desperate scriptwriter in *The Player*, an executive with a talking boil on his neck in *How to Get Ahead in Advertising* and a bisexual fashion designer in *Prêt-à-Porter*. 'If you've got a face the length of a tombstone,' he says, 'you don't play hero roles, I'm afraid. You have to play the odd parts.'

Last year, he earned new credibility with his daughter by playing the Spice Girls' manager in *Spiceworld the Movie*. 'When the part came up, Olivia was elated. She would never have forgiven me if I'd said no. I had to report back every day with a progress report and the best thing was she got the chance to go on set and meet the girls. My rating with her schoolfriends will probably never be as high again...'

Running alongside his acting career, Richard is also developing his talents as an author. His earlier book, *With Nails, The Film Diaries of Richard E. Grant*, shot straight into the bestseller lists and this autumn, as well as seeing the release of *The Scarlet Pimpernel*, also heralds the publication of his first novel, *By Design*, described as a story of sex and interior design.

One film Richard is happy to forget was his first experience of the Czech Republic. 'I made a film there called *The Cool Light of Day*. It was a remake of a 1950s film but

The Pimpernel always goes to great lengths to conceal his identity from his pursuers.

thankfully was never released. Luckily *The Scarlet Pimpernel* was infinitely more pleasurable. Prague looks like every painting or picture you've ever seen of the French Revolution so the background is perfect. But you do long for English caterers and it was nice coming back to film in England, knowing that when you wanted to talk to the extras, you didn't have to go through a Czech instructor.

'The costumes from the period of the French Revolution are the most fantastically flattering clothes. Women can have arses the size of Asia and they can be completely hidden; they can have minute breasts and have them puffed up so that they look like Pamela Anderson. All the men's clothes lengthen your waist and your legs and the corsetted nature makes them very flattering. It helps your posture so that you can't slouch easily. The only things I didn't like were the shirt cuffs, the buckled shoes and the stockings. Having to pull up stockings was a real drag. And you can look great from the waist up until you see legs which look so comical in relation to the rest of the body because they're highlighted by white stockings. I suppose if I had legs like Arnold Schwarzenegger, I'd be more than willing...'

Whereas in the past the Scarlet Pimpernel has always operated by means of a series cunning disguises, Richard reveals that his Pimpernel relies on different methods. 'There are no disguises as such this time,' he says, 'and I must admit I was a little curious about that at the beginning. It seemed to me a radical departure from the way the stories were written where he dressed up as a woman, an old man and so on. But they thought the notion of somebody being able to wear convincingly an eighteenth-century prosthetic make-up wouldn't work – he'd be caught out. So in these films he's a man who lives by his wits and speed rather than disguise. The script emphasises the difference between his two sides – a man who is so effete he doesn't look as if he could punch a marshmallow, but who is perfectly capable of killing someone in two moves without making a sound. The disguise is that he seems like the kind of man who doesn't have a disguise. No doubt aficionados of the book will say: "Where's the old lady with the warts scene?" I felt exactly the same way at first and, to be honest, I'm still not entirely convinced, but they talked me into it. I do occasionally wear a black mask, but the Lone Ranger is about as near as I get to any disguise!

'For most of my scenes, I had a stunt double because of the insurance alone. If I'm on a series for four months, I can't afford to have any situation where I could be seriously injured. So for close-ups of sword fights it's me, but for the wide shots with all the Errol Flynn stuff, it's my double.

'The muskets drove us all to distraction. We might do two takes on a scene with ten pages of dialogue and then nineteen takes because one gun doesn't go off. And there'd be a burning carriage, horses everywhere, people falling out of buildings but because one of the guns doesn't go off, you have to do the whole thing again. I've decided that muskets are the equivalent of cap guns that you had as a kid. Just as you want to shoot someone dead in your garden, they don't go off.

'I've done some riding but anyone galloping in the distance at great speed won't be me! When actors go on chat shows and say they did 99 per cent of their own stunts, I think: "You're just lying." It's also insulting to the stunt people who risk their lives and do an absolutely fantastic job. I rode horses where I grew up in Africa but that's very different from a film where a horse has to stop and there may be gunfire, smoke and explosions. It's not like riding old Dobbin around Richmond Park.

'They put me on a horse called Ebony which literally had to have four sticks of dynamite up his arse before he would move. As soon as he was out of sight of the trainer, he'd think, "I'll just have a jog over here and take a break." They assured me that he would never throw me off.'

Elizabeth McGovern as Lady Marguerite Blakeney

Nothing seems to faze Elizabeth McGovern. At seventeen she was plucked from high school by Robert Redford to appear in his movie *Ordinary People*, so the prospect of giving birth to baby Grace just two months before starting work on *The Scarlet Pimpernel* held no terrors for the American actress.

Opposite: Marguerite has her hair trimmed in readiness for her date with the guillotine.

Below: Elizabeth McGovern describes Marguerite as 'instinctive, impulsive and passionate'.

Thirty-five-year-old Elizabeth, who also has another daughter, Matilda, aged four, says: 'Because I had a nanny, I was able to have Grace around every minute on *The Scarlet Pimpernel* and, to my delight, it was a real asset rather than a handicap for everyone in the crew because she was a diversion. She helps you to stay down to earth, to keep hold of your perspective. So that was nice for me to have a sense of normality because filming is a business with long days and long periods away from home. And I just didn't want to be separated from her.'

The daughter of two teachers, Elizabeth was born in Chicago but brought up in Los Angeles 'where everybody and their aunt either wanted to write a TV play, direct a TV play or be an actress. So I decided that wasn't what I wanted to do but, because that was the business of the town, I did plays at school and I loved it.' Her debut was at fourteen, but it still didn't spark any great longing to take to the stage, partly because she was raised in an environment 'about as far from showbusiness as you could get. I didn't grow up watching movies and absorbing them like mother's milk. Somehow we existed in a world that – even though it was LA – was far from the Hollywood people have perceptions about, especially in England.'

Nevertheless an agent spotted her in a high school production of Thornton Wilder's *The Skin of Our Teeth* and told her to give him a call if she needed work. 'I still didn't know what I wanted as a career but one thing led to another.' She made the call 'thinking I was just auditioning for summer work to go to college' and landed a leading role as Timothy Hutton's girlfriend in *Ordinary People*. 'It is one of those weird things that my very first paying job happened to be in this pretty great movie that was actually also a commercial success. For someone who

kind of fell into acting, I've been very lucky.'

After *Ordinary People*, she decided to enrol at the Juilliard School in New York where her classmates included Kelly McGillis and Kevin Spacey, but gave up the drama course after a year to star as showgirl Evelyn Nesbit in Milos Forman's *Ragtime*, for which she received an Oscar nomination. With hindsight she concedes: 'Maybe for a while I was too much flavour of the month. I was sent countless scripts, whether I was suitable or not.'

Elizabeth continued to work with some of the biggest names in Hollywood – including Robert De Niro (*Once Upon a Time in America*), Sean Penn (*Racing with the Moon*), Dudley Moore (*Lovesick*), Kevin Bacon (*She's Having a Baby*) and Michael Caine (*A Shock to the System*) – and combined her movie work with classical theatre roles on Broadway. In the meantime, she had met a young Englishman, Simon Curtis, through mutual friends in New York while she was dating Sean Penn. She didn't see Curtis again for ten years but in 1993 they married and she moved to England.

'I have always been drawn to England in an emotional and psychological way,' she says. 'I grew up in the San Fernando Valley and yet I was always an Englishwoman among them, even though I didn't know it at the time. It is the reverence for words that I most admire about England. I don't know if that is because I am not from here and therefore I find the language richer and more exotic. I think these are qualities that come from the strong theatre tradition. But it was never a conscious plan to come to Europe and base my working life here. If I had been told that I would end up here with an English husband and two little girls, I wouldn't have believed it.'

By then, Simon Curtis was an accomplished television producer/director and soon cast his new wife in *Tales from Hollywood* and *The Changeling* where she countered any charges of nepotism with outstanding performances. In the latter, she displayed her acting prowess by playing a virgin when she was five months pregnant with Matilda! Her most recent roles include *The Misanthrope* at the Young Vic, *Hurly Burly* at the Old Vic, the BBC adaptation of Arthur Miller's *Broken Glass* and the film *Wings of a Dove*.

For the time being, Elizabeth is happy to be working in England because it means she can spend plenty of time with her husband and daughters, but she certainly hasn't turned her back on Hollywood for good. 'I'd love to be offered a good part in a movie so I really think it would be wise not to write Hollywood off. I worked hard for ten years and just to abandon it is not something that interests me. But most important, beyond making a living, is working on material that I find exciting. Having found myself in a family with two children, I feel stronger and more grounded, I suppose, as a person, which makes me freer to enjoy my work.'

Elizabeth has relished the fresh challenge of *The Scarlet Pimpernel*. 'The title was vaguely familiar to me but it wasn't a book I'd read. However, being involved in the films encouraged me to bone up on the French Revolution which is not taught in as much detail in American schools as it is here. I knew the basic gist and about people like Robespierre but I'd forgotten how closely it paralleled American history at the same time. It was a fascinating period and, as I learned more about it, it dawned on me how closely the fashions of the Revolution mirror the fashions of the 1960s – the big hair, big ear-rings and outrageous clothes. Both were periods of rebellion where the people were taking their fate into their own hands.

'I read books to give me an insight into eighteenth-century France, a background to the sort of place where Marguerite lives. Marguerite is instinctive, impulsive, passionate – typically French – witty and bright...in other words, a delightful part. She wants to be in the middle of the action, right by the Pimpernel's side. She's a very strong personality. I like the complexity of the relationship between Sir Percy and his wife and I think theirs is a very interesting portrait of a marriage. For me, the whole thing of him being the Scarlet Pimpernel becomes a metaphor for trust within a marriage – actually

Portrait of a marriage – Marguerite and Sir Percy.

waking up with somebody you've fallen in love with, and whom you think you know, and looking at them and thinking: "Really I don't know the first thing about you." And also Sir Percy finds out things about her that he never knew. When he's a fop, she wonders why she still loves him, so when she discovers that he is the Scarlet Pimpernel, it's like a rebirth of their marriage. It brings back all the excitement and she remembers why she married him.'

The Scarlet Pimpernel also enabled Elizabeth to renew her acquaintance with Prague. 'I'd been to the Czech Republic before as a tourist, just as the government there was changing in the late Eighties. It was a very exciting time to be there. It was interesting to go back and see how the country had changed, which it has quite a bit. When I was first there, the people were so ecstatic – literally singing in the streets – but now I get a real sense of confusion, a lack of confidence as to how to proceed. Nobody seems sure about the way ahead. But the beauty has always been there. I remember ten years ago that walking through the old town square in Prague was like you were the first person ever to discover it because there were no tourists. The only trouble was, you couldn't get any fresh fruit.

'I adore the costumes that Marguerite wears – they're such wonderful materials and colours. The corsets were uncomfortable but the dresses themselves weren't heavy so it wasn't too arduous. And the wigs were nice and light too. The riding was another great attraction. I love horses and I love to ride. I've ridden since childhood although I've never actually owned a horse. There was a good chemistry between me and my horse on the show, Seamus. He was very good and always hit his mark. Mind you, I was always working on the bond between us with lumps of sugar.'

Martin Shaw as Chauvelin

Martin Shaw was knocked out by his role as Chauvelin – quite literally, after an unscripted scene where he received a blow on the head from his own gun.

'I've ridden for about thirty years but I hasten to add I don't consider myself to be a particularly good rider. When I knew I was going to be doing a lot of riding on *The Scarlet Pimpernel*, I made sure I got to the stables early so that I got the pick of the best horse! The perfect qualities for a film horse are a horse which looks high-spirited and dangerous but in fact responds to control very well. The one thing you don't want is a safe old Dobbin who doesn't do what you tell him. It looks dull and boring. I managed to get a beautiful black horse called Sam and he fitted the bill perfectly. He was very strong and very high-spirited – very masculine but not dangerous.

'Anyway we did seven or eight takes of a scene where I had to gallop down a steep hill and intercept some other galloping horses, then make Sam rear and fire a pistol under his neck. To do that, you don't put charges in the gun otherwise it would upset the animal. All went well, but after about seven takes the ground underfoot got a bit muddy and as I made Sam rear, which I did by just pulling him back a bit, he lost his footing, skidded and threw his head back. His head hit my arm, which was holding the pistol, and that threw the pistol into my head and knocked me out.

'I was momentarily stunned. I fell off the horse, which didn't hurt at all, and stood up immediately. Everybody rushed over, and I said: "I'm absolutely fine." But I wasn't fine – I was only half-conscious after the blow on the head from the pistol. It took me two days to recover...but I didn't take any time off.'

Apart from that mishap, Martin enjoyed the action scenes and would have liked to have done even more sword fighting. 'I've fenced before on TV and in films and whilst

Chauvelin finds himself on the receiving end for once.

I did a bit of fencing on *The Scarlet Pimpernel*, sword master Terry Walsh and I would have liked a bit more time to rehearse. And we lost a lot of time with the muskets. They didn't always go off in real life but people had the luxury of being able to put in a huge charge of gunpowder to make sure they would go off. But we couldn't put in a big charge because it would have been too dangerous. I've got a little trick of my own which I often pass on to other actors who aren't used to guns. When you fire a weapon that fires blanks, there's no recoil; but with a real weapon, there is recoil. So when I fire a blank pistol, I always put in a fake recoil to make it look more realistic.'

Martin admits that he found Baroness Orczy's writing style something of an acquired taste. 'When I was cast as Chauvelin, I wasn't familiar with the Pimpernel books at all so I was lucky in that I came to the project almost completely fresh. I'd seen the Anthony Andrews version on TV so I knew the story but I went out and bought the book anyway because I enjoy research. I like the preparation part of the job very much – in this case, I enjoyed immersing myself in the feel of the age. To be honest, I didn't find the book much help as far as research was concerned because I don't think Baroness Orczy really cared very much. Not having read it, I thought it would be like *Les Misérables* or *A Tale of Two Cities* but it's really not in the same league so we're very fortunate that Richard Carpenter has done such a good job with the adaptation. To be perfectly frank, it's not a very good book. But the script is excellent.

'I read a bit about the history of the French Revolution. My father-in-law is a real heraldic and historical expert and I found out from him that there was a real Chauvelin – although his name was Bernard not Paul – and that he was the Ambassador to the Court of St James at the time of the Revolution. So that's where the Baroness must have got the name.'

Martin disputes the theory that the public aren't used to seeing him as a villain, pointing out that his roles cover a wide range. 'I like playing villains because villains don't wake up every morning – unless they're psychotics – and think: "Who can I screw up today?" They think what they're doing is right and so when you're playing someone who is a villain, you've got to like him and you've got to believe in what he stands for. That's the fun.

'Chauvelin still loves Marguerite. In the book, he was an out-and-out villain, but in the script we give him some reason for the way he behaves. It makes more sense from a modern perspective because his convictions are political. He is the eighteenth-century equivalent of the Workers' Revolutionary Party or any extreme group. In another age, he would have been a key member of the Khmer Rouge or Hitler's right-hand man. He is somebody whose background as a rich bourgeois was very unhappy and the political ideals of the Revolution gripped and excited the young Chauvelin before it went completely wrong. So he is a political idealist with a bit of a chip on his shoulder from his past, but he hasn't completely lost the grace and manners of his upbringing which

Chauvelin at the helm, masterminding another plan to snuff out the Scarlet Pimpernel.

are always at odds with the coarse violence of the Revolution. The pity about the French Revolution is that they didn't find a point of equilibrium because you had the obscenity of the aristocracy treating the peasants appallingly and that was replaced by the violent obscenity of the Revolution. Chauvelin was originally trying to create a true egalitarian state.'

Martin agrees with Richard E. Grant about the fashions of the Revolution. 'The costumes are sensational,' he enthuses. 'They're so good to wear. Howard Burden rang me and asked me to come and see the costume he had in mind for Chauvelin. But he said: "Nothing is set because it doesn't work for me if you don't feel comfortable in it." I thought it was such a nice change to be consulted like that – it was like a partnership. As it turned out, Howard and I had exactly the same idea. He showed me an engraving of the French painter David and said: "That's what I want Chauvelin to look like." It really was a marvellous age. The men's style was called *déshabillé* (meaning slight undress) and that's how I like to dress anyway – loose around the neck.'

It is a popular misconception that Martin Shaw's career dates from *The Professionals* in 1977. He had actually made his television debut ten years earlier and was already an established and highly respected actor by the time the part of Ray Doyle came along. He was born in Birmingham in 1945. His mother was a former champion ballroom dancer, his father an industrial salesman. On his own admission, the only subjects at which Martin excelled at school were English and drama, but he didn't

Martin Shaw studies a playback of his latest scene.

Martin Shaw employed a trick of the trade when firing a gun loaded with blanks.

really consider becoming an actor at that stage. Instead it was assumed that he would follow in his father's footsteps until he miserably failed the necessary exam and opted for acting. At eighteen, he was accepted by the London Academy of Music and Dramatic Art.

One of his first TV roles, in 1968, was as hippie commune leader Robert Croft who took over an empty house in *Coronation Street*. That same year, he played Horatio to Richard Chamberlain's *Hamlet*. After a stint as Welsh student Huw Evans in the popular TV comedy *Doctor in the House*, in 1971 he played Banquo in Roman Polanski's film of *Macbeth*. The parts continued to flow. In 1972, he starred in *Helen, a Woman of Today* before returning to the stage, first with the National Theatre and then in the West End as Stanley Kowalski opposite Claire Bloom in *A Streetcar Named Desire*.

Any fears that *The Professionals* might have typecast him in action roles have proved unfounded. On stage, he won rave reviews for his portrayal of Elvis in *Are You Lonesome Tonight?* and on television he has played such diverse characters as Jack Butcher in Dennis Potter's *Cream in My Coffee*, Sir Henry Baskerville in *The Hound of the Baskervilles*, ill-fated Antarctic explorer Captain Scott in *The Last Place on Earth*, Chief Constable Alan Cade in four series of *The Chief* and English adventurer Cecil Rhodes in the BBC's *Rhodes*.

Playing the young Rhodes was Martin's own son Joe, one of three children by first wife, actress Jill Allen. The others, Luke and Sophie, have also followed their father into an acting career. Martin is now married to his third wife, writer Vicki Kimm.

Filming *The Scarlet Pimpernel* in the Czech Republic brought back frightening memories for Martin of a previous trip there in 1973 to film *Operation Daybreak*. He recalls: 'The only airline that could fly into Prague twenty-five years ago was Aeroflot and you had to fly from London to Paris and change planes. I know about flying – I'm a qualified pilot with my own wartime biplane – and I was sitting behind the cabin bulkhead facing backwards, looking down the cabin with the passengers facing forwards, and as we took off from Paris I thought, this angle of attack is too steep. Then from behind me in the control cabin I heard the stall-warning klaxon going off. I thought, "Oh my God!" Then I felt it stalling and, even though the plane was pointing upwards, I could feel in the pit of my stomach that it was stalling. Immediately the engines came on to full power to try and recover. With the noise and the vibration of the plane trying to fly again, I looked down the cabin and there were all these people looking at me, shouting and screaming, absolutely terrified. Luckily we managed to pull through, but it was a pretty hairy experience and for a while I really thought it was the end.

'When I was in the Czech Republic before, it was during the Russian regime. I'm a vegetarian – I have been for thirty years – and there was no Czech word then for vegetarian. It was something they didn't understand. I spent three months out there in the middle of winter eating nothing but pickles and bread and cheese. It wasn't even decent bread and cheese, but hard, semi-stale bread and processed cheese. It was very difficult. So I approached this time with some caution, only to find that there is now a word for vegetarian in Czech – *vegetarianska* – and that there are vegetarian restaurants and health food shops in Prague. And the food now is delicious.

'The change in the city as a whole is breathtaking. It was so oppressive the last time I was there that you didn't notice how beautiful Prague was. There was no colour there before because they were literally only allowed six dyes for their clothes. And there was no advertising, no neon signs – it was pretty dreary. But now the place is full of light and music.'

Martin also found that he was fondly remembered by the Czech people from *The Professionals*. '*The Professionals* is still very fresh to the Czech people – it was one of the biggest things ever to have hit them. I think it's because they got it at a time when their liberty was taken away and so it was a symbol to them of western freedom and resistance. Now they've got their freedom and the programme has been repeated. So wherever I went, people approached me – very polite and very dignified but extremely starstruck – with calls of, "Bodie, Doyle". It's nice to know that the programme meant something to people during such a difficult time.'

Anthony Green as Sir Andrew Ffoulkes

Anthony Green is still pinching himself. It was only five years ago that he suddenly decided to take up acting after rejecting careers in medicine and law and in that short space of time he has found himself working opposite actors of the stature of Sir Derek Jacobi, Richard E. Grant and Martin Shaw.

Blackburn-born Anthony left school at eighteen with the intention of studying medicine, but after two years at medical school he failed the exam and turned to law instead. He went to Nottingham University and, although he duly graduated in law, he had, on his own admission, been more interested in the university drama society and in productions at the Nottingham Playhouse. Among the university plays in which he appeared were *The Crucible*, *Look Back in Anger* (as Jimmy Porter) and the production which made Richard E. Grant's career, *Withnail and I*.

'Going to the Nottingham Playhouse inspired me,' says Anthony, 'and as soon as I qualified as a lawyer, I decided I wanted to be an actor! My mum took a job with Marks and Spencer to help pay for me to go to drama school and I was lucky enough to get into the Academy of Live and Recorded Arts (ALRA) at Wandsworth where there is a flourishing television department.

Sir Andrew Ffoulkes (Anthony Green) is attracted to Suzanne de Tournay (Beth Goddard).

The Pimpernel's faithful sidekick – Sir Andrew Ffoulkes.

'After that, I had small parts in *Pie in the Sky* and *Where the Heart Is* plus two lines as a naval officer in the Bond movie *Tomorrow Never Dies*. But my big break was being cast as Berenger, the sidekick of *Cadfael*. There I was, just a year out of drama school, working with Sir Derek Jacobi. We had ten weeks in Budapest and I had plenty of good scenes with him. It was wonderful experience, just watching and learning from such an accomplished actor.

'When I auditioned for *The Scarlet Pimpernel*, I knew the story and I'd seen the Leslie Howard film on TV years ago, but I hadn't read the book. So the moment I got the part, I put that right. I also bought some history books on the period and, when I discovered that Sir Andrew lives in Pall Mall, I spent an afternoon wandering around the area, just to get the feel of the place.

'I didn't want to make Sir Andrew too dashing. Whilst he is utterly loyal to the Pimpernel, I didn't think he should be fearless. He leads a great life in England but he wants to help out in France and that is what drives him. Really he's perfectly normal and knows that every mission is a matter of life and death – usually his.'

Anthony, who is twenty-eight and single and whose other TV credits include *A Wing and a Prayer* and an episode of *Wycliffe*, adds: 'I had to do quite a few action scenes in *The Scarlet Pimpernel*. I'd done a bit of riding on *Cadfael* so I knew my way around a horse. I wouldn't say I'm a particularly good rider, but I'm better than I was. Luckily, the horse was fine – a real professional. I also did fist fights and a spot of disarming and fired a few muskets in anger. But I had to change my grip because when I first picked up a musket, I held it like Bodie and Doyle did in *The Professionals*. I was informed that if I didn't change my grip, I would burn my fingers when the thing went off. I didn't have to be told twice...'

Denise Black as Gabrielle Damiens

Denise Black is prepared to be even less popular with viewers than when she played wayward hairdresser Denise Osborne who dumped Ken Barlow in *Coronation Street*. 'It's true that dark-haired actresses get to play baddies and my character in *The Scarlet Pimpernel* is definitely a baddie.

'I had great fun as Gabrielle or, as she came to be known, Mademoiselle Guillotine. I was forever riding around hitting people, chopping off people's heads on horseback. I had to hit Elizabeth McGovern virtually before being introduced to her. And she'd just had a baby! The only trouble was I got my head blown off in the end so there's not much chance of my being in a sequel.

'For my very first scene, I had to get off my horse (accidentally leaving most of my clothes still on the horse) and hit the butler with my glove. The butler was played by a huge Czech extra who towered over me so that I had to stand on tiptoe to hit him! And because he didn't speak a word of English, I was a bit worried about upsetting him, so when we were rehearsing I said to the translator: "Could you please explain to him that I'm not actually going to hit him?" It was late at night and something like minus eight when we did that scene and we all huddled around fires to keep warm. But this guy had a wet suit on underneath his butler's costume because he had to end up in the water and the heat from the fires began to melt the rubber. He smelt really odd.

'After all the smacking I'd done, I asked whether I could punch or kick for a change, so that was nice. And I had a wonderful time torturing Robert Langdon Lloyd who plays the saintly Father Joseph. He's a lovely man and we got on so well that although his character was bleeding profusely from a head wound which Gabrielle had just inflicted, we played a word game between takes. So, you see, it was nothing personal...

'Gabrielle is a home-grown girl,' continues Denise, 'whose family are dead and she just gets caught up in the action. But she's got a chip on her shoulder and that prompts her ruthless behaviour. She is a fiercely ambitious leader who is all in favour of rape and pillage – even at a convent. And there were female sansculottes because the principle of sexual equality did operate during the French Revolution.

'I had worked for director Patrick Lau three times in the past – on *The Adventures of Sherlock Holmes*, which was my first TV, on an episode of *The Bill* and on the Screen Two film *Dead Romantic*. So I was delighted when he cast me as Gabrielle and I immediately started reading up on the French Revolution. Also a friend of mine, Pam Gems, had written a play, *The Snow Palace*, which featured Danton and Robespierre so I went to watch that to pick up some tips. Funnily enough, Martin Shaw's daughter, Sophie, was in it. In the end I modelled myself on Gerard Depardieu's film portrayal of Danton. I also did some research into the guillotine and discovered that it had originally been introduced for humanitarian reasons, to create equality. Apparently the idea of such an implement was thought up to enable all of the people to die in the same manner because previously the aristocracy had enjoyed a much cleaner way of death than the poor. So the guillotine was seen as a great leveller, particularly of necks.

'Most of Gabrielle's clothes were made specially. I wore a tricolour skirt which was hitched up for riding – it was her idea of a uniform – with various royalist trophies dangling from the buckles. Howard Burden found a picture of an authentic ear-ring which consisted of a Revolution hat on the ear-piece and suspended below that was a tiny guillotine and then below that was the king's head severed at the neck. So he had

Denise Black as the fiercely ambitious Gabrielle Damiens.

a copy made up for Gabrielle to wear.

'Apart from the corsets, which make it almost impossible to eat lunch, the only other problem was the military greatcoat which Gabrielle wore. This made getting on and off a horse a major deal. Steve Dent took us to his farm at Rickmansworth to train us but whilst I have ridden in the past – I once galloped across the Andes in the 1980s with an actors' touring company – I belong to the cling-on school of riding. I'm the kind of rider who wonders when I'll fall off. At first, I was given a nice quiet horse but it didn't like the reflection of water so they gave me the same horse as Elizabeth McGovern with a bit of extra polish on it to make it look different.

'My new horse liked to gallop but was fine. I played it safe. When I did a scene where I had to trot my horse down through a cobbled arch with fifteen Czech extras on horseback, I said to actor Robert Perkins, who is a very good horseman, "I'm sticking with you." And for anything too risky, they used doubles. There is a scene with

Gabrielle riding along a treacherous, slippery road with a sheer drop down to a lake on one side. Well, that's not me. I leave that to the experts – people like Richard E. Grant's double, who is a brilliant acrobat on a horse.

'I was supposed to whip someone on horseback, but the horse bolted at the sign of the whip so I got cold feet and the whip scene was cut. But the funniest time was when I'd finished a speech and the horse went on to the next scene. I had to be brought back, much to the puzzlement of the Czech extras.'

In company with the rest of the cast, Denise had her fair share of traumas with muskets. 'I was taught how to fire a musket and not to go "Oooh!" when it suddenly goes off. That was the trouble with them – they were so unpredictable. You can pull the trigger and nothing happens, then you try again and there is a mighty bang with fire and smoke coming out of the barrel. I wore ear-plugs. And some of the guns were about four feet long and very heavy. I could hardly lift them.'

Ironically, in view of all her action scenes, Denise's worst injury was sustained at a local disco. 'It was immediately after Gabrielle had been fatally shot. I emerged unscathed from that but that night I went out dancing with Richard E. Grant and the make-up girls. All the local Czech girls were much taller than me and I ended up being accidentally elbowed in the eye. So the next day I reported on set with a big black eye and Pam Haddock had to cover it up because it was for a scene where I was supposed to look my best.

'Although I got nice looks from wandering around all day *déshabillé*, I also suffered in my seduction scene with Richard. It was the end of a long day and Richard thought it would be fun for the Pimpernel to play with Gabrielle sexually with a napkin and then stuff it in her mouth before tying her up. Not only couldn't I keep the wretched napkin in my mouth, but I finished up with a carpet burn on my chin and bruises on my elbows. It can be dangerous playing a dangerous woman.'

Emilia Fox as Minette

'The most important thing about the French Revolution was learning how to keep your head,' laughs Emilia Fox. 'And that's where Minette's duplicity stems from. It's the survival instinct, looking after number one. She's not a femme fatale or an obvious villain but chooses the Republican side out of necessity because it seems the safer option. I think she'll surprise a few people.

'I remember from doing 'A' level history what a fascinating period the French Revolution was and I've always been a huge fan of *The Scarlet Pimpernel*. I read the books as a child and have always watched any Pimpernel films on TV and now that I'm in this production, my nephew and younger brother are really excited about it.

'The women of the Revolution were ahead of their time concerning fashion and got to wear the most fabulous hats. And they often had their hair cut very short in a guillotine look. Before people went to the guillotine, they had to have their hair cut and the Republican women used to have theirs cropped deliberately. They were taking the mickey out of the guillotine and thought it was safe to do because they were on the Republican side. So, for Minette, I had two distinct looks. When she's in actress mode, I wore this high red wig and heavy make-up. But when she is herself, my hair was cropped and my make-up suggested innocence.'

The daughter of Edward Fox and Joanna David, Emilia (or 'Millie' as she is known to all) is one of our brightest young actresses. Coming from such an acting dynasty, it might have been assumed that Millie would automatically go into acting, but she preferred to keep her options open. 'As I got older, I thought acting might be fun to go into but I wanted to go to university first and have the opportunity to broaden my mind. My parents never tried to influence me one way or the other. They knew that if it was something that I wanted to do, then fine. As soon as I got to Oxford, I set up a company with some friends and we started doing classical plays like *A Midsummer Night's Dream*, *The Glass Menagerie* and *The Seagull*.'

While still at Oxford, Millie played Georgiana Darcy in the BBC's acclaimed production of *Pride and Prejudice* and then, immediately after taking her English finals, she started rehearsals as Mrs de Winter in the ITV adaptation of Daphne du Maurier's *Rebecca*, opposite Charles Dance and Diana Rigg. 'It was an unbelievable week. I did an exam in the morning at Oxford before rushing to London for the read-through on *Rebecca* in the afternoon! I then drove back and had to revise for my exam on the Romantics the next day. I stayed up all night on that and then went into my last exam on the Thursday. It was all very exciting although I was in a bit of a daze by the end of the week. Luckily, I got a 2:1.'

Millie has hardly had time to draw breath since. She played Anya in the Royal Shakespeare Company production of *The Cherry Orchard*, starred in *Bright Hair* for the BBC, Catherine Cookson's *The Round Tower* for ITV and earlier this year filmed *The Trilogy* for Stephen Poliakoff. And she recently landed the plum role of Henry VIII's fifth wife Catherine Howard in a major new play about her ill-fated life.

Given that Catherine was beheaded, *The Scarlet Pimpernel* proved ideal preparation. 'It was lovely filming in Prague for six weeks. It was the first time I had ever been there and I managed to get the chance to go sightseeing. Although Minette met a grisly end, I didn't have to do any action scenes but I did see a lot of people jumping out of windows. My most nerve-racking scene was in the tiny theatre at Litomysl where I had to stand on stage and perform a play in front of all these Czech extras. They couldn't have understood a word I was saying – they must have thought I was mad.'

Emilia Fox dons a big wig to portray Minette in actress mode.

CHAPTER EIGHT

PIMPERNEL '98

EPISODE ONE

France, 1780: At the Château Saint-Cyr, two children are forced to watch as their parents are executed on the orders of the Marquis de Saint-Cyr to set an example to his rebellious peasants. This incident, plus other similar atrocities committed throughout the land, helps spark the French Revolution.

Opposite: At first, Marguerite has no idea that her husband is the Pimpernel.

France, 1792: With the country gripped by revolutionary fervour, three mysterious cloaked figures lead a group of people out of Paris to safety. At the Palais de Justice, agent Chauvelin, acting upon the authority of the Committee of Public Safety, is interrogating an Englishman, James Danby, in an attempt to extract information about the infamous Scarlet Pimpernel. Meanwhile Armand Saint-Just flees to his lover, Minette, an actress at the celebrated Théâtre des Arts. Armand and Danby are both members of the League of the Scarlet Pimpernel, a dedicated and courageous team led by an unknown English aristocrat, whose daring rescue missions are an embarrassment to the Republican government. Robespierre, the political head of the government, is putting pressure on Chauvelin to destroy the League and the Pimpernel himself.

Below: The ill-fated Danby (Dominic Mafham).

Sir Percy Blakeney, one of the richest men in England, a leader of fashion, accomplished sportsman and a man renowned for his flamboyant wit, is the Scarlet Pimpernel. Alerted to Danby's capture, he recruits his right-hand man, Sir Andrew Ffoulkes, and snatches Danby from under Chauvelin's nose, but in the course of the raid Percy is wounded by a bullet fired by Chauvelin. The rescue proves in vain. Danby, weak from torture, fails to survive the journey back to England, but

Danby gives a death-bed warning to the Pimpernel.

before he dies he warns the Pimpernel not to trust a certain woman. She remains unnamed.

In England, a ball is being held to mark the birthday of the Prince of Wales and among the guests is Lady Marguerite Blakeney, Sir Percy's beautiful French wife, from whom he is currently estranged. Also in attendance is Suzanne de Tournay, one of those rescued earlier. She is an old friend of Marguerite's and they speculate excitedly as to the identity of the Scarlet Pimpernel. Marguerite has no idea that they are talking about her husband. Chauvelin is present too, as part of his bid to ensnare the Pimpernel. He has ordered the arrest of Armand, Marguerite's brother. Marguerite is wary of Chauvelin: during her days as an actress, they were once lovers.

Percy conceals his secret identity behind his public persona and recites a little ditty of his own composition about the Scarlet Pimpernel. Suspicious of the connection between his wife and Chauvelin, he invites the latter to be their guest at Blakeney Hall. Another of the French emigré guests, Angèle Saint-Cyr, accosts Marguerite and slaps her across the face. Percy defends his wife's honour but, on their return home, it emerges that the couple's estrangement is linked to the Saint-Cyr family. Marguerite was accused of having denounced them, causing Angèle's family to go to the guillotine.

At Blakeney Hall, Chauvelin watches a cricket match and blackmails Marguerite into revealing the identity of the Scarlet Pimpernel in return for her brother's safety. She begs Percy to help in some way and explains how the Marquis de Saint-Cyr executed her parents – she and Armand were the two children at the château – adding that

Chauvelin had tricked her into supplying him with information which led to the Saint-Cyrs' downfall. Aware that their conversation is being overheard, Percy tells Marguerite that he is unable to help Armand. The next morning, Marguerite sees Percy wince as he mounts his horse – a wound he had previously attributed to a fencing accident.

Chauvelin puts the heat on Marguerite. All she can remember is the address of a safe house in Paris used by the League; Suzanne had recognised it as belonging to their old singing teacher. Chauvelin offers a possible clue to the Pimpernel's identity: during their last encounter he was grazed by a bullet. Remembering her husband's wound, Marguerite rushes to Percy's study. On his desk, a wooden engraving of the scarlet pimpernel flower releases a secret drawer containing maps of Paris. She now realises that Percy is the Scarlet Pimpernel and that she has just betrayed him to Chauvelin.

In Paris, Percy recruits Minette to help them discover in which prison Armand is being held. They arrange to meet the following day at the Café Mechanique. Marguerite has followed her husband to Paris to warn him but, on entering the city, her fake identity is blown and she is arrested and brought before Chauvelin. Suspecting that Sir Percy Blakeney is the Scarlet Pimpernel, Chauvelin is certain that an imprisoned Marguerite will prove the ideal bait to trap the Pimpernel. Later, Chauvelin receives a visit from Minette.

At the Café Mechanique, Minette tells Percy that Armand is being held at La Force prison. The café is then overrun by Chauvelin and his men. Percy manages to escape but not before another League member, Lord Tony, is killed by a bullet intended for his

Far left: Chauvelin's henchman Fumier (Chris Fairbank).

Left: Marguerite's brother Armand (Pascal Langdale).

Minette's smile soon vanishes as her treachery is uncovered.

leader. Reunited with Sir Andrew and Minette, Percy reveals his plan to use a secret tunnel in La Force to rescue Marguerite and Armand. Minette promptly heads straight for Chauvelin.

Chauvelin dispatches a team of soldiers, under the supervision of his sidekick Fumier, to search La Force and find the tunnel. With the search party busy in the dungeons, Percy holds the prison governor at gunpoint and secures Armand's release. Allowing himself to be arrested, Percy demands to see Marguerite and the pair are reconciled in his prison cell. Percy then sets about freeing himself from solitary confinement using instruments concealed in a special coat customised by Planchet, a tailor who is a League member. He escapes just as a bloodthirsty mob storms the prison, killing everyone in its path. He battles his way to Marguerite's cell, only to find it empty.

Marguerite is brought before the revolutionary tribunal. Chauvelin had never meant this to happen and tries to defend her against Minette's denunciation, but to no avail. Marguerite is condemned to death. The tumbril sets off with its prisoners towards the guillotine with Chauvelin leading the procession. En route, a drunk lurches into its path, causing the driver of the tumbril to pull up. A blazing cart rolls out from a side street, separating Chauvelin from the prisoners. The League ambush the tumbril and Percy defeats Chauvelin. Later at the theatre, Minette's dresser finds her with her throat cut. But Marguerite is safe in the arms of Percy, the man she now knows to be the dashing hero – the Scarlet Pimpernel.

EPISODE TWO

The Vendée region of France is in the grip of civil war. Republican troops, acting on the orders of local leader Gabrielle Damiens, otherwise known as Mademoiselle Guillotine, are destroying the entire area, a centre of Catholic and royalist insurrection. When their château comes under Republican attack, the Marquis de Rochambeau and his daughter, Helene, are helped to escape by their family priest, Father Joseph. However, Helene is too ill to flee to England and takes sanctuary in a convent. Her father continues his journey but promises that he will return for her.

In England, Rochambeau seeks out Marguerite, an old friend from Paris, at Blakeney Hall and arrives during an engagement party for Suzanne de Tournay and Sir Andrew Ffoulkes. Rochambeau begs Percy to ask the Scarlet Pimpernel to rescue Helene, adding that his gamekeeper, Carnot, will be able to direct the Pimpernel to the convent.

Chauvelin is in disgrace and has taken to the bottle. He is to be sent to the town of Cholet in the Vendée, an area in which he grew up, to find Helene de Rochambeau so that Robespierre can use her as a bargaining tool against the Marquis who is stirring up anti-revolutionary support in England. To flush out Father Joseph, and thereby find Helene, Gabrielle Damiens resorts to the ruthless tactic of guillotining five innocent people a day. Father Joseph listens in anguish as the blade takes its first victim.

En route to Cholet, Chauvelin and his men stop at a farmhouse to water their

Left: Helene de Rochambeau (Julie Cox), Chauvelin's long-lost daughter.

Centre: The kindly Father Joseph (Robert Langdon Lloyd).

Below: Vanel (Robert Perkins), Mademoiselle Guillotine's second in command.

Mademoiselle Guillotine cracks the whip.

horses. The owner, Carnot, advises them of a safe haven for the night. Later he tells his wife that he recognises Chauvelin as Valentin Gaultier who left the Vendée under a cloud some twenty years earlier.

While Father Joseph reluctantly turns himself in and gives Damiens the information she needs, Percy, Marguerite and Andrew arrive at Carnot's farm. He draws a route map to the convent but then reveals the details to Chauvelin. However, before

Chauvelin can carry out his surprise attack, his men are ambushed by a band of rebels, led by a young aristocrat known as Monsieur Henri, who shoots all visible survivors in cold blood. Only Percy's intervention spares Chauvelin. Henri takes them as prisoners to the rebel camp in the heart of the forest where Percy explains that, as a special agent of Robespierre, Chauvelin is more useful alive. Chauvelin is thrown in with the pigs and Percy is released.

In the town square in Cholet, a crowd watches as Father Joseph is guillotined. Damiens and her men set out for the convent. Marguerite gets there first but learns that Helene has vanished. Instead she is at the rebel camp as Henri's lover. Damiens arrests Marguerite and takes her back to Cholet but only after ordering the slaughter of the nuns. While Henri plans to avenge the nuns' deaths by attacking Cholet, Chauvelin argues with Helene about Republican principles. As she reveals details of her past, it dawns on Chauvelin that he is her real father. Once Helene is out of sight, Fumier, the only other Republican to survive Henri's ambush, manages to free Chauvelin.

In Cholet, Percy and Andrew stride in to Damiens' office and announce themselves as Chauvelin and Fumier. She has been expecting them. Percy warns her that an English spy and his French wife may also be looking for Helene whereupon Damiens orders the guard to fetch Marguerite. Brought before Percy and Andrew, Marguerite plays along with the deception so that when the real Chauvelin and Fumier arrive, Damiens thinks they are impostors and has them taken to the cells.

Alone with Percy, Damiens wastes no time in seducing him. He seems happy to oblige before seizing the opportunity to bind and gag her. It wasn't quite what she had in mind. He then secures the release of Marguerite and Andrew and the trio escape from Cholet in a hail of bullets.

Percy has deduced that Helene must be with Henri and heads for the rebel camp. He berates Henri for not being honest about Helene's whereabouts, but Helene insists that she loves Henri.

The rebel assault on Cholet proves disastrous. Tipped off by Fumier, Damiens is lying in wait. Helene impulsively decides to join the battle and seeks out Henri. As she runs across the battlefield, Chauvelin orders the soldiers to hold their fire but it is too late – she has already been hit. Henri too is wounded and dies in Helene's arms. Chauvelin races over to his daughter and carries her to safety but Percy assumes that she has been snatched and gives chase, as does Damiens. Percy holds Chauvelin at gunpoint as Helene staggers over to him. Then Damiens trains her gun on Percy but, before she can fire and much to Percy's amazement, Chauvelin shoots Damiens dead and tells Percy to get Helene to England. Percy, Marguerite, Andrew and Helene ride out of Cholet but Helene's injuries are too serious and she is unable to continue. Reassured by the love of Rochambeau and of Henri, Helene dies in a clearing in the woods. Chauvelin's ghost is now laid to rest.

EPISODE THREE

As orphans of the *ancien régime* are being indoctrinated with Republican ideals at a high security institution on the outskirts of Paris, a ten-year-old boy stands out from the rest. He is Louis Capet – the Dauphin, heir to the French throne. Whilst the other boys sleep, a particularly zealous warder, Monsieur Jouvin, enforces the Dauphin's catechism, denouncing his parents and the monarchy. They are unaware that a masked intruder has broken into the building and Madame Jouvin is unable to save her husband from the intruder's attack or to prevent the Dauphin from being carried away.

Sir Percy Blakeney is performing his courtly duties at Carlton House, entertaining the Prince of Wales. The Dauphin's Swedish physician, Baron Valdemar, is also present. He is concerned about the boy's poor state of health but has been denied access to the child. A disparaging comment from Percy provokes a fierce and public row between him and Marguerite which ends with her announcing that she is leaving him and Percy receiving a humiliating rebuke from the Prince for not being able to control his wife. All of this is observed by a French Republican spy.

Arriving back in France, Marguerite is met by Chauvelin, who escorts her to Paris for an interview with Robespierre. She affirms her allegiance to the Republic and agrees to Robespierre's suggestion that she can best serve the Republic by returning to the theatre. Percy too arrives in Paris, secure in the knowledge that Marguerite is now in

Sir Percy entertains the Prince of Wales...or vice versa.

the hands of the Republican authorities from whom she should be able to gather vital inside information. For their separation was a sham – part of a grander plan to rescue the Dauphin. But first they need to find the boy and to discover who has taken him.

Robespierre receives a ransom note demanding a large sum of money in return for the Dauphin. He is desperate to keep the boy's disappearance a secret since the Dauphin is a crucial bargaining tool in the war with Austria. Besides, if the Committee of Public Safety were to learn of Robespierre's carelessness, it would surely signify the end of his political career and no doubt his life. Chauvelin assures Robespierre that the matter is in hand.

Robespierre (Ronan Vibert), the orchestrator of evil.

Marguerite is introduced to La Touraine, the leading actress and *grande dame* of the Théâtre des Arts. Marguerite is to perform an epilogue to the current play, a production written by Robespierre himself to serve as blatant propaganda for France's war effort against her European neighbours. La Touraine barely manages to conceal her fury at this proposal.

Percy and the League have a lead on the Dauphin – a man called Calumet. But they find him dead: murder concealed as suicide. They have better luck when they find Madame Jouvin working in a laundry. She is clearly terrified of them, but Percy assures her that he is the Scarlet Pimpernel and will arrange for her safe passage out of France in return for information about the missing Dauphin. She describes the intruder's red executioner's mask, strength in snapping her husband's neck and brilliant swordsmanship. But no sooner has she imparted this information than Madame Jouvin is ruthlessly silenced.

While Percy is convinced that the Dauphin has been abducted rather than taken by royalists, Baron Valdemar makes another appeal to Robespierre for access to the boy. The request is denied and a warrant is issued for Valdemar's arrest.

Marguerite prepares for her performance at the Théâtre des Arts. She is dressed as Liberty and begins reciting Robespierre's speech, but when it meets with scorn from the audience, she addresses the people as herself, making an impassioned plea to defend liberty as their birthright. The audience bursts into tumultuous applause; they hoist her on to their shoulders and carry her triumphantly from the stage. La Touraine is seething.

In a desperate bid to raise money for the war effort, France holds an auction of the dead king and queen's possessions, attended by representatives of the very countries she is at war with. Among the guests are Chauvelin and Percy, who is attracted by a silver

Designer Tim Hutchinson's drawing for the set of the Théatre des Arts.

box bearing an inscription to Marie Antoinette from the Chevalier d'Orly, a notorious spy and assassin who was said to have been the queen's lover before apparently dying of the pox in Turkey. Later, Marguerite arrives at the auction and makes a great show of throwing her wedding ring at Percy, a scene witnessed by both Robespierre and Chauvelin. The pair then learn that the Scarlet Pimpernel has freed Valdemar – confirmation, in Robespierre's eyes, that Sir Percy cannot possibly be the Pimpernel since he was at the auction the entire day. Chauvelin hopes that the marital split will enable him to rekindle his romance with Marguerite.

Stumbling across La Touraine being dressed as a man by Cecile, her devoted dresser, a suspicious Marguerite searches the star's dressing-room and discovers the red executioner's mask worn by the Dauphin's abductor. Marguerite and Percy believe that La Touraine is also the Chevalier d'Orly, but what they don't know is that she/he is working for Chauvelin, who has uncovered La Touraine's secret identity and masterminded the kidnapping. Chauvelin learns that Marguerite has been spying on La Touraine and realises that her rift with Percy is a fake. At the theatre that night,

Chauvelin traps Marguerite.

Meanwhile La Touraine instructs a waiting cab driver to take her to a deserted château. The driver is Percy. On the way, she changes into the Chevalier but Percy follows her into the château where the Dauphin is being held. In a desperate sword fight, Percy outwits the Chevalier who, in frustration, impales herself on Percy's sword. Just as Percy is about to leave with the boy, Chauvelin appears holding Marguerite as hostage. Percy bluffs his way around Chauvelin's threats to kill Marguerite, giving her the opportunity to disarm her captor.

Chauvelin takes the Chevalier's dead body as proof to Robespierre and clears himself of any involvement in the kidnapping, laying the blame squarely on the dead assassin. He also tells Robespierre that he discovered the Dauphin dead but has found a look-alike replacement. Robespierre's secret will remain intact. Meanwhile, back at Blakeney Hall, Andrew is teaching the Dauphin to play cricket. The boy knows he will never be king but Marguerite muses that one day there won't be any kings. Percy wonders if his wife has the gift of prophecy...

A LEAGUE OF THEIR OWN

Cast

Role	Actor
Sir Percy Blakeney	Richard E. Grant
Marguerite	Elizabeth McGovern
Chauvelin	Martin Shaw
Sir Andrew Ffoulkes	Anthony Green
Fumier	Chris Fairbank
Minette	Emilia Fox
Gabrielle Damiens	Denise Black
La Touraine	Suzanne Bertish
Armand	Pascal Langdale
James Danby	Dominic Mafham
Robespierre	Ronan Vibert
Prince of Wales	Jonathan Coy
Suzanne de Tournay	Beth Goddard
Mazzarini	Ron Donachie
Planchet	Gerard Murphy
Fisher	Milton Johns
Henri	James Callis
Rochambeau	Peter Jeffrey
Marquis de Saint-Cyr	Andy De La Tour
Father Joseph	Robert Langdon Lloyd
Helene de Rochambeau	Julie Cox
Valdemar	Jerome Willis
Carnot	Alex Norton
Lord Tony	Jamie Bamber
Thouret	Campbell Morrison
Solange	Diana Payan
Vanel	Robert Perkins
Mother Superior	Edith MacArthur
Comte de Claris de Florian	Richard Dempsey
M. Jouvin	Stuart Fox
Mme Jouvin	Sarah Berger
Auctioneer	Philip Fox
Gaston	Bryce Engstrom
Dauphin	Dalibor Sipek
Cecile	Winter Uhlarik
Figaro	Karel Roden
Suzanne	Petra Kulikova
Felix	Jiri Hanak
Committee member 1	Dan Rous
Committee member 2	Pavel Chalupa
English gentleman	Robert Carruthers
English lady	Nancy Bishop
Man in audience	Robert Orr
Executioner	Mike Cella
Spy	Slabodan Milovanovic

Crew

Executive producers	Tony Virgo
	Johan Eliasch
	Hannah Rothschild
	Morgan Mason
Producer	Julian Murphy
Line producer	Kevan Van Thompson
Directors	Patrick Lau (1, 2)
	Ed Bennett (3)
Head of production (Birmingham)	Trevor West
Production executive	John Greening
Writer	Richard Carpenter
Script editor	Jill Raistrick
Designer	Tim Hutchinson
Director of photography	Simon Kossoff
Music	Michael Pavlicek
Costume designer	Howard Burden
Costume supervisor	Jill Shaw
Make-up designer	Pam Haddock
Make-up assistant	Alison Davies
Casting director	Andy Pryor
Casting (Prague)	Nancy Bishop
Production co-ordinator	Sara Hamill
Production secretary	Caroline Holder
First assistant director	Edward Brett
Second assistant director	Sarah Dibsdall
Art directors	Desmond Crowe
	Hayden Matthews
Prop buyer	Mike Smith
Editors	Jeremy Strachan (1, 2)
	Andrew McCelland (3)
Choreographer	Bruno Tonioli
Stunt co-ordinator	Steve Dent
Sword master	Terry Walsh
Camera operator	Julian Barber
Focus puller	Adam Gillham
Clapper loader	Sean Cobbley
Grip	Steve Evans
Gaffer	Eddie White
Sound mixer	Clive Derbyshire
Boom operator	Peter Margrave
Continuity	Maggie Lewty
Finance assistant	Maria Hurley
Publicity	Wendy Dickinson
	Matthew Robinson